D0295100

WITHDRAWN

The Z/Yen Group

Z/Yen Group Limited
5-7 St Helen's Place
London EC3A 6AU
Tel: (020) 7562-9562
Fax:(020) 7628-5751
Email: hub@zyen.com

Business Forecasting Using Financial Models

How to Use the Key Techniques
of Financial Modelling to
Interpret Business Proposals

NEIL HOGG

FINANCIAL TIMES

PITMAN PUBLISHING

PITMAN PUBLISHING
128 Long Acre, London WC2E 9AN

A Division of Longman Group Limited

First published in Great Britain 1994

© Neil Hogg 1994

British Library Cataloguing in Publication Data
A CIP catalogue record for this book can be obtained from the British Library

ISBN 0 273 60529 1

No responsibility is accepted by the author, BDO Consulting or the publishers
for any loss occasioned to any person acting or refraining from acting as a
result of material in this publication. All names in this book are fictitious.
Any resemblance to the name of any existing person, business or company is
purely by chance and is quite unintentional.

10 9 8 7 6 5 4 3 2

᾿set by PanTek Arts, Maidstone, Kent
d and bound in Great Britain by
\Ltd, Guildford and King's Lynn

᾿hers' policy is to use paper manufactured from sustainable forests.

CONTENTS

PREFACE

This book is about simulating business processes in financial terms, using computer systems, commonly referred to as financial modelling. Financial models are often responsible for the evaluation of major business decisions. Despite this, the models that support these decisions are often either inadequate in their representations of underlying business processes or they contain major errors of logic or execution. Experience of complex financial modelling projects across a wide variety of economic sectors suggests that there are four principal reasons for this failure:

- poor understanding of economic and financial analysis
- inadequate planning and poor design of models
- insufficient discipline in structuring models
- incorrect interpretation of model output.

Much of the boom in financial modelling in the 1980s and 1990s resulted from the use of spreadsheets. Although spreadsheets are now the *de facto* standard for financial modelling, they are also one of the prime reasons why so much financial modelling has encountered problems. Thus, although much of the discussion in this book is independent of the software selected to carry out modelling, the focus will be on spreadsheets.

This book is divided into four parts, reflecting the problems outlined above. Part I concentrates on two areas. First, it presents a classification and analysis of current approaches to financial modelling and synthesizes these to produce a recommended approach. Second, it considers the use of techniques of financial evaluation, such as net present value, both with and without risk.

Part II looks at model planning and design. It begins by presenting an approach to evaluating the requirement for a model and then reviews data collection and analysis before considering the content of model logic.

In Part III, the emphasis switches from a business-focused view to the techniques required to build a model on the computer. The first chapter in this section looks at the selection of computer systems. It then lays out the basic principles of good modelling and reviews model-building techniques before concluding with an examination of model quality control.

Part IV concludes the book by considering the use of models in practice, based on a detailed, worked example of a real-life project and an examination of the problems with using models as an aid to decision making.

Finally, I would like to thank colleagues at BDO for their help in developing ideas and reviewing parts of the manuscript.

Part I

BASIC PRINCIPLES

1

INTRODUCTION

WHAT IS FINANCIAL MODELLING?

The term financial modelling is widely used to describe a spectrum of analytical methods. The common theme of these is the representation of business processes in numerical terms on a computer. Applications of financial modelling vary from the complicated and business-critical, such as corporate planning and acquisition analysis, to the straightforward and routine, such as monthly cash monitoring. Some of the most common applications of financial modelling include:

- capital project appraisal
- assessment of strategic/business options
- evaluation of financing structures, including merger and acquisition opportunities
- cost reduction planning
- market planning
- bid evaluation
- forecasting of cashflow, profit or asset base
- human resource planning.

At first sight, the models required for each of these applications may seem very different, but, on closer inspection, a number of common features can be identified. This results in four main types of model:

- *option evaluation using relative criteria* this sort of model rates previously identified options against each other, for example, if a number of projects have been put forward for central approval by divisional management, a model may be used to rank the proposals and, thus, make a selection
- *option evaluation against absolute criteria* in practice, purely relative evaluation is unlikely as there must also be some absolute measure of 'goodness', for example, if all of the projects submitted by divisions have

a negative net persent value (NPV), it would be undesirable to authorize any of them (an example of a common absolute criteria is a hurdle rate for the internal rate of return (IRR))

- *option identification* in some cases, the business options may not have been fully identified before modelling begins, in which case, one of the main reasons for using a financial model is to provoke thought about what the options are
- *optimization* the final type of model is used to analyse one option in greater detail, for example a human resources planning model may be concerned with identifying the minimum staff cost for a given work forecast.

PROPOSITION

There are a number of tools available to the financial modeller, both in terms of software and hardware. For example, large multinationals may use mainframe computers running suites of models developed using specialist modelling languages. Other companies – of lesser means or more modest aspirations – may use spreadsheet software running on personal computers (PCs).

A few years ago, there would have been little dispute that the multi national using a specialist modelling language would have been running a larger and more complicated model than the company with the PC and spreadsheet. Today, however, the same may not be true. PCs are now very powerful and the spreadsheet software they run has developed over many years' use, much of it involving building and running financial models of some kind.

The increased availability and power of spreadsheets has opened up many opportunities for improved financial modelling. Indeed, the use of financial modelling is now much more widespread than it was 10 to 15 years ago as a direct consequence of this. Although spreadsheets offer many advantages, they are, like certain brands of fast sports cars, highly dangerous in the hands of the uninitiated. The main danger with spreadsheets is that their ease of use and the rapid feedback they provide positively encourages ever greater complexities and nuances to be incorporated into models. Often, the hope is that this will provide 'insight' into the business issue being studied. Unfortunately, though, the result is more frequently hopeless confusion.

Complicated models that add little value are worryingly commonplace. In order to understand *why* this is so, it is necessary to consider the different approaches to financial modelling that are commonly observed and the pressures under which financial modelling takes place. This is examined next.

The lessons of this analysis are then combined to construct a hybrid approach to defining the appropriate role and content of financial models.

APPROACHES TO FINANCIAL MODELLING

Although the preparation of a financial model is seen as an essential part of many business decision-making processes, there does not seem to be one, generally accepted view of what constitutes financial modelling. There are two main issues that cause particular disagreement. The first is whether a model must describe the world through algebraic relationships in order to be a true model. For example, is a model really a 'proper' model if all it does is take cost and sales information and reorder that data into financial statement format, or must the model contain expressions for the relationship between, say, output and variable costs to be thought of as a model?

To take another example, consider the following two models. The first inputs projected sales over the next 12 months from an interview between the modeller and a sales director. The second uses an equation derived by multiple regression analysis from examining the past five years' sales data. Many people, particularly from technical backgrounds, contend that only the latter example can truly be thought of as a model. The counter argument is that the sales director effectively has the same information as the regression model inside his head and, although he might conceptualize the problem in a different form, his own analysis gives similar results. If this assertion is accepted, then the two approaches can be seen as comparable, that is, both are models. It is a question of whether the model resides *explicitly* on the PC or *implicitly* in managers' heads.

The second area of disagreement about what constitutes a financial model is to do with whether models should concentrate on representing accounting relationships, such as profit = sales – costs or whether the model should also explicitly model economic variables, such as the structure of markets, the availability of substitute products, technological change, economies of scale, the maintenance of barriers to entry and so on. Because these are difficult variables to model, they are often excluded from the analysis.

Both the above problems are to do with how far the relationships within a model should attempt to explain reality. The alternative to explicitly modelling reality, in all its complexity, is to examine more complicated issues using a less structured medium (such as management workshop, task forces, research projects and so on) and to confine the model to supporting these other methods (that is, carrying out the arithmetic).

These may seem academic and rather fruitless debates, but it is important to think of the model as just one part of a wider evaluation process. For example, if a company wishes to build, own and operate a new power station, it must certainly examine the full raft of economic issues, such as the level and variability of demand for power, fuel prices, competition and so on. Also, in order to satisfy senior management, bankers and investors, the firm will clearly have to produce financial forecasts. It has a choice, though, over how much of the viability analysis to drive through the financial model and how much by other means.

There is, potentially, a substantial cost involved in getting this balance between financial modelling and other means wrong. If insufficiently detailed modelling is carried out, there is a danger that analysis will be superficial: data may be taken for granted, the exact mechanisms of business processes insufficiently thought through and impacts on cash, profit and so on inadequately analysed. The opposite side of the coin – an overly ambitious model – can be as bad or worse:

- the modelling tools chosen may prove inadequate
- data may not be available at the necessary level of detail
- not enough may be known about the relevant relationships (such as how advertising spend affects sales) in order to model them properly.

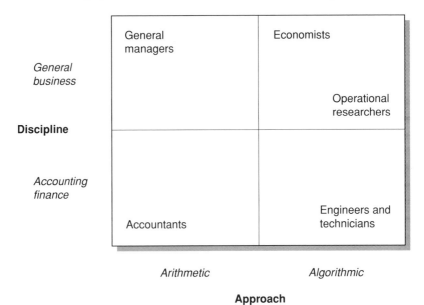

Figure 1.1 Approaches to financial modelling

All of this may result in the model being unable to produce anything of value at all.

Unfortunately, there is no magic answer to the question of where to apply financial modelling; it is a balance. Where exactly the balancing point is will vary, depending on the requirements of individual projects.

To a large degree, different approaches to financial modelling have become associated with the different groups of people who typically become involved, such as accountants, economists, engineers and technical people, operational researchers, general managers and planners/strategists. Figure 1.1 summarizes the approximate position of these groups. To help illustrate where financial modelling can be used most effectively, two of the main views of its role are now examined in more detail below.

The Pragmatist's Approach

Most financial models are developed and used by accountants. By its nature, financial modelling requires some knowledge of accounting and this has come to mean that it is most commonly an accountant who will be the modeller. Many of those in senior management in British business are also trained accountants, and those who are not certainly require a sound knowledge of the subject. Few senior businessmen are economists or operational researchers, although some are engineers by training. The result is that the view of, and approach to, financial modelling adopted by accountants is extremely influential and can be considered the dominant view of the subject in the UK.

The characteristics of this approach to financial modelling are:

- *PC spreadsheet-based* the increased availability of cheap, powerful and easy to operate spreadsheet packages for PCs in the 1980s opened up the possibility of non-computer people developing and running complicated financial models, and accountants were a key group in taking advantage of this
- *financial statement-driven* the objective of financial models is seen to be to produce the standard statements of balance sheet, profit and loss and cash flow, possibly together with a number of key performance indicators
- *non-optimizing* with this approach, models do not attempt to output one optimal result because of the complexity of modelling the necessary relationships
- *deterministic* it is uncommon to find such models explicitly building in a range of probabilities for variables such as sales – typically, multiple-sensitivity analyses will be conducted to examine the behaviour of the output in different scenarios

- *tautological and not algorithmic assumptions* the assumptions entered into this type of model tend to be primarily simple accounting relationships, such as profit = sales – cost, so the model is primarily arithmetic.

This view will, hereafter, be termed the Pragmatist's Approach.

The Pragmatist's Approach keeps the model computationally simple and focuses on carrying out the arithmetic that might previously have taken place on large sheets of analysis paper. The model is, therefore, a means of presenting a body of input data in a commonly understandable format and allowing straightforward manipulation of these results. However, this is not to say that these models cannot be both large and complicated.

This approach is viewed by many as the most suitable role for a financial model. It avoids the necessity to model complicated economic variables and to model directly uncertainty. The process of building the model is seen as a prompt for thought and discussion about the issues facing the business. The less deterministic aspects of the problem will probably be tackled via less analytical means.

Detractors of this approach argue that using a model in this way is time consuming and adds little of intrinsic value. They argue that an alternative approach to provoking thought is often more effective, such as management workshops or brainstorming. Other groups argue that it is right for the model to take a central role, but that the model must itself add value to the analysis by incorporating probabilities and by accepting the challenge to incorporate realistic economic relationships. These people might be labelled the Theorists.

The Theorist's Approach

Business is a subject with a rich theoretical underpinning that encompasses many disciplines such as psychology, economics and mathematics. Of these disciplines, the one of most direct interest to financial modelling is economics. Therefore, just as accountants can be most closely associated with the Pragmatist's Approach, economists are most often linked with the Theorist's Approach.

Economists and accountants have a long sparring history. Accountants often see economists as overly theoretical and insufficiently aware of commercial reality, while to economists, key accounting concepts, such as depreciation, are anathema. Not surprisingly therefore, economists' models tend to take a rather different approach to accountants'.

This tension between economists and accountants is further heightened by two differences in their respective modelling heritages. The applied branches of economics have traditionally relied on mathematics and statistics for their modelling tools. Mathematics – and particularly differential calculus – is primarily used to find the optimal solution to problems. It is applied to the study of problems such as finding the equilibrium number of firms in a given market, optimization of profit under monopoly or the profit maximizing amount for a firm to spend on advertising. The use of statistics (and particularly regression analysis) in economics is known as econometrics. Econometrics forms the basis of much of economists' empirical work, whereas mathematics is used to a greater extent, but not exclusively, for theoretical work. Unlike economics, accounting has made little use of mathematical methods until recently. The second difference in heritage comes from the greater role of theory in economics. This too has had an effect on the economist's approach to modelling.

In the fairly recent past, most financial modelling was fairly simple and was carried out on sheets of analysis paper by accountants. Nowadays, the issues that organizations expect to address using financial modelling are often much more complicated, such as determining corporate competitive strategy and assessing the impact of different regulatory regimes. These problems are areas in which people trained as economists and working in fields such as merchant banking, management consultancy and business planning often become involved. Although traditional economic analysis can be applied to these problems, a simulation approach, such as financial modelling, may offer the only possibility for analysis of real-world complexities. The Theorist's Approach brings together the economist's approach to analysis with the simulation approach of financial modelling. The Theorist's financial model may be characterized as follows:

- *not confined to PC environments* the analysis traditionally used by economists has often made use of powerful midrange and mainframe machines using specialist statistical and analytical software and this heritage still has an influence: people following this approach will often use a specialist modelling package, such as FCS, in place of, or in addition to, spreadsheets
- *goal driven* whereas the Pragmatist's Approach focuses on producing traditional financial statements, the Theorist's Approach is directed more at examining the impact of assumptions on a few key variables, which might be profit measures, but might equally be variables such as market share or the height of barriers to entry
- *complicated assumptions* with this approach, more of an attempt is made to achieve optimal solutions, such as the profit maximizing price, and to

ascribe probability functions to variables in order to take account of chance factors, so the relationships in the model will also be more complicated, resulting from the need to model economic relationships.

The Theorist's Approach, therefore, makes greater use of relationships built into the model itself to give explanatory power to the modelling process, as opposed to using the model more as a prompt, as in the Pragmatist's Approach.

Other approaches

In between the Pragmatists and the Theorists there is clearly a fairly broad spectrum of other possible approaches. Indeed, it is even too sweeping a stereotype to say that accountants are Pragmatists and economists Theorists – these are merely handy labels for the approaches that are evident in business. In addition to those mentioned already, a third important group of people also become involved in financial modelling in business. These are the technical people, such as operational researchers, engineers and scientists. As might be expected, their approach is, in many ways, quite close to the view of the Theorist, as it places greater emphasis on the model and less on the process than that of the Pragmatists. The distinguishing factor between these two approaches lies more in their focus: the theorists focus on economic relationships, the technicians perhaps more on physical relationships, such as machine efficiency and resource usage.

PRESSURES ON FINANCIAL MODELLING

Anyone who has been involved with even a moderately large financial modelling exercise will know that there are constant pressures on the modelling process. The approaches discussed above often flounder because they fail to recognize these pressures. This section considers a number of them so that the basic Pragmatist's and Theorist's Approaches can be modified accordingly.

Stakeholders

By definition, financial modelling in business is an important and high-profile activity. This means that there are stakeholders in the modelling process, for example, senior strategic and functional management, planners, finance staff, regulators, key investors, non-executive directors and strategic partners.

There are two important consequences of this breadth of involvement in the modelling process. The first is that different stakeholders will be involved in specifying the model and in building and running it, which can lead to confusion and poor communication. Typical problems include failing to specify the objectives of the modelling process properly and failure to project manage the process. Both these will lead to increased development times.

The second consequence comes from the fact that stakeholders can be divided into two groups: those that are involved in some way in developing the model ('developers') and those for whom the output of the model is intended ('audience'). Much of what the developers are striving for will be determined by what they perceive the requirements and expectations of the audience to be. These expectations may sometimes lead to a desire to deliver the results that managers believe these groups want to see rather than a more objective picture. Of course, this may not always be intentional, but it can arise merely from a desire to see only what they want to. It may also lead to what might be called the 'spurious complexity' of some models: that is, to models that appear highly sophisticated superficially, but in reality make more use of complicated algorithms than good business sense to achieve the desired results. This might also be familiar as the 'blind them with science' or the '200-page printout' approach.

Adding value

Naturally, models are under a constant pressure to contribute something positive to the study of which they are a part. This involves two, potentially conflicting, elements: delivering results quickly and adding greater insight into the issues that the organization faces. The dilemma that this poses can be seen in the typical development cycle of a Pragmatist's model. The modelling process commonly starts with a simple model, designed to act solely as a support to the planning process. However, as time goes on the temptation to try to add complexity in order to add 'insight' grows. The model begins to sprawl and, if proper controls are not adhered to, can quickly become bogged down.

Training

Financial modelling is effectively now a discipline of its own, building on skills in accountancy, economics, finance, computing and mathematics/statistics. Despite this, there are few texts and little training that cover all the required skills in the modelling context. The result is modellers who produce badly designed and, therefore, unreliable models, who run over time and budgets and who fail to recognize the business issues that they should be taking account of in the modelling process.

Communication

It comes as a surprise to many new to financial modelling to discover that, as well as offering an insight into the inner workings of business, modelling can be a fast track to career disaster. Financial modelling is often a highly political activity, due to its importance in planning and budgeting. As such, modelling may easily become one of the pawns in battles for office supremacy. Open communication and a determination to articulate and evaluate all important assumptions are the most effective tools for the financial modeller to use in sidelining such behaviour.

Two examples of the importance of communication in modelling can be seen. The first is to prevent models being used to discredit a particular group in the organization. This technique may be employed by a person or group frightened of the change that the model's results may cause. One tactic employed is to follow the progress of the model closely, but not become associated with it, then launch a campaign of criticisms based on the knowledge that has been built up. This can either be done in the open, or via personal contacts behind the scenes. The importance of modelling, coupled with its intrinsically iterative nature, make this a very effective, but highly negative, form of office politics.

Open communication is also important in stifling attempts to 'use the model to prove what we want it to'. Most commonly, this is used by subsidiaries to try and gain approval for their capital projects. The techniques used vary, but the objective is normally to include a combination of scenarios and variables that push their projects over the required hurdle rates of return. The model then ceases to be a tool for maximizing corporate returns and becomes, instead, a force of sub-optimization.

CONCLUSIONS: A SYNTHESIS OF APPROACHES

The approaches of both the Pragmatist and the Theorist have much to commend them. The Pragmatist's Approach offers a way to provide a financial view of strategy. The Theorist's Approach aims to provide a greater insight into the workings of the business in its competitive environment. Nevertheless, neither approach offers any reasonable guarantee of adding significant value to the planning process and neither adequately addresses the pressures on modelling referred to above. The Pragmatist's Approach relies on some, unspecified, process of applying a simple model in order to focus thought and generate ideas. The Theorist's Approach, on the other hand stands a significant chance of becoming bogged down in the complexity of its own aspirations. The next section will discuss some of the lessons that can be learned from both approaches.

Appropriate role of the financial model

Financial modelling will always be a fairly time-consuming process. Indeed, as many organizations have discovered, this is one of its principal problems. Clearly, the benefits of building and running a financial model must outweigh the costs involved in its construction. Deciding when to use financial modelling must, therefore, involve a consideration of where models can add most benefit. The question of whether that benefit can be better, or more cheaply, obtained by other means can then be evaluated.

The basic purpose of using any model is to try and construct a representation of the real world for the purposes of experimentation. Models, such as the financial models that we are concerned with here, are known generically as mathematical models because they represent the world through a series of equations. Mathematical models are widely used outside business. For example, in aircraft design, as an alternative to wind tunnel testing, use is increasingly made of hugely complicated models of aerodynamics that are run on super-computers. In a field such as aircraft design, the model means that the effects of changes in designs can be more quickly, effectively and cheaply examined than by other methods.

The analysis typically carried out in business is significantly less mathematically demanding than in fields such as engineering. This means that business has the option, for most analysis, of using qualitative techniques such as brainstorming or panels of experts in place of, or in support of, computer modelling. Financial models do, however, provide important benefits:

- combining financial and non-financial information in a common (that is, financial) format, for example, the model to examine the viability of a new power station might include sections looking at technical issues, such as turbine efficiency and the energy value of fuels, economic issues, such as the impact of competition on the electricity price, and financial issues, such as the cost of finance and the depreciation of assets
- allowing the impact of a change in one variable to be seen on the bottom

line and, thus, facilitating the development of multiple scenarios, so, to take the power station example once more, the effects of using coal from different countries, each coal having a different energy value, delivery schedule and cost, can be evaluated

- provoking thought – the focus of most business is financial and, as such, seeing a situation represented in financial terms often allows managers to gain a better 'feel' than being presented with the same picture in qualitative terms
- allowing the financing requirement to be sized, depending on assumptions such as the timing of capital payments, the rate of revenue build-up and the funding instruments available to the project.

Appropriate content of the financial model

The above benefits appear to make a good case for the use of financial modelling. The question is, therefore, what sort of model is required to realize them. There are, perhaps, two broad approaches to answering this question. The first approach is to build a fairly simple, Pragmatist's model and then use it to run sensitivity analysis. The second approach is to incorporate economic variables and probability into the model itself.

The sensitivity approach is the most common and has two stages: first to establish a base case (the most likely or preferred scenario) model and then to run a number of sensitivities (or variations) on key parameters of the model. For example, if a model assumes that a selling price of £1.49 is a suitable base case, sensitivities might be run to see the effect of prices ranging from £0.99 to £1.99.

Sensitivity analysis is easy to carry out, but can be criticized on a number of grounds, including the following:

- the range of sensitivities run is frequently without basis. In the example above, it is more than likely that the best and worst cases would have been chosen at random, simply to be round numbers
- sensitivities are typically run on a *ceteris paribus* basis, that is, one variable is changed while all others are held constant. It is then difficult to assess the impact of several together because the relationships between the sensitivities is not known. To get around this problem some people suggest taking all the worst case scenarios and running them together – a disaster scenario. However, to do so is not always realistic. For example, sensitivities may have been run on interest rates and on inflation. The worst case scenario might show interest rates rising from 8 to 15 per cent

and inflation rising from 3 to 15 per cent. However, although this may seem plausible, it suggests a cut in real interest rates from over 5 to 0 per cent – an *improved* position

- running 100 rather than 2 sensitivities on a variable involves 50 times as much work, but gives no better idea of what might most realistically be expected to happen.

Addressing these criticisms involves three stages. First, modelling relationships as accurately as possible. For example, in the case of inflation and interest rates given above, it might have been better to forecast starting values of both variables and then project forward using real interest rates. Second, it is usually preferable to assess the probability distribution of key variables rather than to run sensitivities. That way, one – expected value – result can be obtained. Third, data and relationships should only be incorporated into the model where they are:

- *significant* the likelihood of error in a model increases proportionally much faster than the size of the model increases, so it makes sense to keep the model as small as possible – for example, if it is known that power costs are affected mainly by production volume, but also by job mix and working patterns, then it will often be preferable to keep the relationship programed into the model simply between power cost and production volume
- *measurable* it seems obvious to say that relationships should only be included where they can be measured, but, nevertheless, it is not uncommon for a lack of firm data to be compensated for by invention and the use of tautological relationships.

The concept of measurability can be taken further if the data used in a financial model is thought of as falling into one of three broad types:

- *macro* such as gross national product, inflation, base lending rates, average family expenditure, unemployment, technology and currency exchange rates
- *market* such as market size (money value or number of customers), number of competitors, price/availability/acceptability of substitute products, level of barriers to entry, average customer income and demand elasticity
- *organizational* including cost structure and level, productivity, management structure, product innovation, pricing policy and production processes.

In general terms, models should avoid including forecasts of macro variables for two reasons. First, these variables are outside the firm's control and, second, evidence shows that the forecasts are likely to be wrong and so using no forecast is an as good, or even a better, strategy. Models should include all material market variables, as these will have a significant impact on almost any project, and all material organizational variables.

Final thoughts

As can be seen, there are no hard and fast rules as to what financial modelling should be used for and what a model should look like – much will depend on the pressures of an individual situation. None the less, the broad rules discussed above should always be kept in mind. What can always be done, and what will always pay dividends, is to adopt a rigidly disciplined approach to developing models and to make sure that the model that is built is correct. These issues form the content of the rest of the book.

2

BASIC FINANCIAL EVALUATION

INTRODUCTION

Financial models usually have two types of output. First, they show a picture of the relationships and flows in the business, such as working capital, sales, costs, financing, capital expenditure and so on. This is ultimately expressed in the traditional financial statements of balance sheet, profit and loss account and cash flow. This enables managers to gain a feel of what is going on and to assess the dynamics of the business by, for example, looking at the impact of a competitor's price cut. The second output is to assess, in some way, the health of the business. This latter goal is usually achieved by means of the calculation of some index of profitability. It is this second output that is focused on here.

There are many different evaluation methods in use. They may be classi-fied in two main ways:

- discounted versus non-discounted measures
- profit-based versus cash-based analyses.

An example of a non-discounted measure is the return on capital employed (ROCE), whereas a discounted measure is net present value (NPV). ROCE is based on accounting profit figures, whereas NPV is calculated from cash flows, that is ignoring accounting adjustments such as depreciation. For a number of reasons (outlined below and explained in greater detail in the books given under further reading at the end of this chapter), the main focus of the discussion here will be on the use of discounted cash flow (DCF) techniques.

Although DCF techniques, such as NPV, are widely used and are often critically important to the future of projects, they are frequently incorrectly applied. This may seriously distort the quality of the decisions they support. The principal objective of the overview of financial evaluation contained here is, therefore, to lay out how to apply DCF correctly in four main areas:

- choosing the appropriate DCF tool to use
- defining the cash flow to discount
- setting the discount rate to use
- managing risk.

A BRIEF INTRODUCTION TO DISCOUNTING

What is discounting?

Most financial appraisal is concerned with evaluation over more than one time period. Typically, this will involve spending some money now in order hopefully to make profit some time in the future. For example, an advertising agency wishing to expand into Europe may have calculated that its initial investment – in terms of buying offices, establishing local contacts and so on – will be £350 000. In this example, the agency is a partnership and, therefore, the money will be raised from a cash call on the partners. The partners estimate that their revenues will average £300 000 a year for the first 3 years and that to achieve this level of income they will have to spend £175 000 per year. They therefore forecast £125 000 a year profit. Should the agency go ahead?

At first sight, the deal, while not looking fantastic, does not appear to be too bad. At these profit levels, the partners will have their investment returned to them in under three years and, from then on, it is clear profit. However, consider what else the partners could do with their money. They could, for example, put it into the bank and earn, say, 8 per cent per annum. In this case, they would have £440 899.20 at the end of 3 years[1].

What the partners in the advertising agency really need to know is whether they would be better investing their money in the bank, this project or somewhere else entirely. Discounting provides the means to do this, by taking the opportunity cost (also referred to as the 'time value') of money into account. The time value of money can be thought most simply as the amount of money that would have to be given up if resources were invested in a given project rather than deposited in the bank.

Before going on to explain how discounting works, it is worth scotching a common misconception. The concept of the time value of money is entirely separate from the question of inflation. None the less, inflation is still an important consideration in finanical evaluation as £100 received now is worth more than £100 received next year, because inflation will reduce the spending power of a £100 between now and next year. These topics can be incorporated into the discounting approach, though, and this will be looked at later.

How does discounting work?

Discounting can be thought of as the opposite of compounding (as in compound interest). To illustrate this more clearly a few terms must be defined.

Present value

Present value (PV) can be defined as the amount of money that would have to be received now that, if invested at a given rate of return (called the discount rate, i) for t periods, would produce an amount, C_t, in t years' time. The formula for this is:

$$PV(C_t) = \frac{C_t}{(1 + i)^t}$$

Example What amount of money received today is equivalent to £500 in 5 years' time if the interest rate is 15 per cent?

$$PV \ (£500) = \frac{£500}{(1.15)^5}$$

$$= £248.59$$

This answer is the PV. If the rate of interest were to rise, less money would be required now as it would grow faster. For example, in the above case, if the rate rose to 18 per cent, only £218.55 would be required now.

Net present value

NPV is an extension of PV to situations where there are more than one cash flow and where these cash flows are both negative (money being spent) and positive (money received). The equation is:

$$NPV = \sum_{t=o}^{t=n} \frac{C_t}{(1 + i)^t}$$

Table 2.1

		Year			
Cash flow	$t = 0$	$t = 1$	$t = 2$	$t = 3$	$t = 4$
Capital expenditure	100		30		
Receipts		24	72	88	72
Operating expenditure		26	38	44	38
Scrap value					30

Example Should the following project be undertaken at a discount rate of 10 per cent (assume that the project is wound up at the end of $t = 4$)?

$$\text{NPV} = \frac{-100}{1.1^0} + \frac{(24 - 26)}{1.1^1} + \frac{(-30 + 72 - 38)}{1.1^2} + \frac{(88 - 44)}{1.1^3} + \frac{(72 - 38 + 30)}{1.1^4}$$

$$= -21.74$$

The project should be rejected as the NPV is less than zero. This is the standard decision rule for NPV: accept only those projects where the NPV is greater than zero. Following this rule will lead to the acceptance of only those projects in which the firm will be earning a greater return than it could elsewhere. An alternative interpretation is that only those projects that give returns greater than the cost of funding (at its simplest, the interest rate) will proceed.

Future value

The future value (FV) is the amount of money that would be received in t years' time if a given sum, C_t, were invested at a specified return, i. This process is what most of us know as compound interest. This is the equation

$$\text{FV}(C_t) = C_t (1 + i)^t$$

Example How much would £400 earn if it were invested at 12.5 per cent interest for 10 years?

$$\text{FV}(£400) = £400 \, (1.125)^{10}$$
$$= £1298.93$$

And just to prove that FV is the reverse of PV (assuming 10 per cent interest over 5 years):

$$\text{FV}(£100) \quad = £100 \, (1.1)^3$$
$$= £133.10$$

$$\text{PV}(£133.10) = \frac{£133.10}{(1.10)^3}$$
$$= £100$$

Why use cash and not profit figures?

We said above that NPV and other discounted methods were always based on cash, not profit, figures. Time will be spent later discussing exactly which cash figures to use, but for now, it is important to realize why NPVs cannot be calculated based on profits.

The profit figure that appears in the financial and managerial accounts of firms represent cash payments and receipts – either actual or expected – adjusted to take account of a number of generally accepted accounting principles. To illustrate one of the most fundamental of these consider a service that has been received but not yet invoiced or paid for, such as electricity. The accounting concept of 'matching' says that, as the use of this service has been received, the profit figure for that period must reflect that use. The profit and loss account will, therefore, be adjusted to include an estimate of the amount used in the period, even if it has not yet been paid for. The concept of depreciation is similar. As far as basic accounting is concerned, an asset reduces in value over time and, therefore, a portion of this cost should be charged against profit each period.

Accounting profit figures provide a handy way of assessing the year-on-year performance of a firm, assumed to be a going concern. However, to use these figures for DCF would produce distorted results. Consider the following example.

Example An entrepreneur is thinking of establishing a small airline offering cheap flights between London and Edinburgh. He has discussed his plans with an airline consultant and they have agreed that two aircraft would be required, at a cost of £15 million each. They would have a life of 10 years, after which they could be sold for £2 million each. The depreciation charge on a 'straight line' basis would be £1.3 million per aircraft, that is (15–2)/10. The consultant advises that each aircraft would make £2 million profit per year, after all costs had been paid. Assuming a discount rate of 10 per cent and ignoring risk and inflation, should the entrepreneur go ahead?

If profit figures were used to evaluate the project the result would be as follows.

Year 1	Profit before depreciation	£4.0m
	Depreciation	(£2.6m)
		£1.4m
Year 2	'Profit'	£1.4m
⋮ ⋮	⋮ ⋮ ⋮ ⋮ ⋮ ⋮	
Year 10	'Profit'	£1.4m
	NPV	£8.6m

If cash flows were used, however, the results would be as follows.

Year 0	Capital expenditure	(£30m)
Year 1	'Profit'	£4m
Year 2	'Profit'	£4m
⋮	⋮	
Year 10	'Profit and scrap'	£8m
	NPV	(£3.88m)

The reason profit figures should not be used is because they are not *real* flows of money. The reality is that the £30 million cost of the aircraft is not available to invest elsewhere and so an opportunity cost must be attributed to this fact. The accounting figures imply that the £30 million is only 'spent' gradually, so overestimating the NPV.

TYPES OF DCF TOOL

So far, one major DCF evaluation tool has been mentioned – the NPV. The NPV decision rule (that projects offering positive NPVs should be accepted and those that do not should be rejected) has also been introduced. NPV does, however, have a number of practical difficulties that have limited its greater acceptance. For example, the choice of an appropriate discount rate for the NPV calculation can be quite complicated. NPV is also perceived by many managers as a rather artificial concept and, therefore, not one suited to real-life business.

One method often proposed as a means of getting round these problems is the internal rate of return (IRR)[2]. The IRR is defined as the discount rate at which the NPV would be zero. It is, therefore, a percentage. Because it is a percentage, it apparently finesses the difficulty of having to pre-define a discount rate. Unfortunately, this benefit is more illusory than real because the IRR decision rule is to accept those projects where the IRR is greater than some cut-off point, such as the bank interest rate. In other words, establishing the cut-off point for the IRR poses exactly the same problems as setting the discount rate in NPV.

The major real benefit of IRR is that managers appear to feel more at home with a percentage measure. The IRR has the additional benefit that it may be compared with interest rates or other measures, such as the firm's cost of capital, and this is found both intuitive and useful. Nevertheless, caution is necessary if IRR is not to be confused with the accounting return measure ROCE – a surprisingly common error.

Whatever is made of these practical pros and cons, NPV is widely considered more theoretically correct than IRR. There are several reasons for this:

- *IRR ignores the size of projects* consider the following two projects (both lasting 5 years and using a 10 per cent discount rate):

  Project 1 capital cost £200 000, annual cash flow £60 000
  Project 2 capital cost £6 666 400, annual cash flow £2 000 000

  both projects have an IRR of 15.24 per cent, but Project 1 has an NPV of £27 447 and Project 2 an NPV of £915 174, so the IRR does not help in making the choice, whereas NPV says that it is better to make £915 000 than £27 000
- *there may be multiple IRRs* Descartes' rule states that there can be as many different IRRs as there are changes of sign in the cash flow and a lot is made of this problem in some textbooks, but, in reality, while it *does* occur quite frequently, it is usually obvious which IRR to choose – if it is not, then there are various methods that can be used to modify the calculation and avoid multiple solutions, but nevertheless *not* using IRR alleviates the need for intricate fixes
- *NPV can cope with changes in the discount rate over time – IRR cannot* again, although a lot can be made of this problem, in practice few people seem to bother using different discount rates each year
- finally IRR also has the rather strange characteristic of, in some circumstances, giving the same result to radically different cash flows, for example, using a 10 per cent discount rate:

  Cash Flow 1 – 700 + 800 + 632 (IRR = 68.02 per cent; NPV = 550)
  Cash Flow 2 + 700 – 700 – 800 (IRR = 68.02 per cent; NPV = –598)

When taken all together, the difficulties with the IRR method are quite serious, and therefore IRR must be considered an inferior tool to NPV. There are further choices, however. Payback is a popular non-discounted method.

 The payback method works by comparing the cumulative sum of the net operating cash inflows so far received by a project against its initial capital cost. When the inflows exceed the outflows, the project is said to have 'paid back'. The lack of discounting means that this method ignores information, and so it has been suggested that the cash flows are discounted before applying payback. However, while this is an improvement on the standard payback method, all cash flows beyond the end of the payback period are ignored. If payback were used in place of NPV, some rather strange decisions might be arrived at. For example, nuclear power stations look quite attractive until the billions of pounds in decommissioning cost, which lie beyond the discounted payback period, are taken into account.

In light of the problems of other discounted methods, the rest of this book will adopt NPV as the standard tool of financial evaluation.

DEFINING THE CASH FLOWS TO USE WITH NPV

It was said earlier that financial models serve both as descriptive/presentational tools *and* as evaluation tools using NPV or an equivalent. Experience would suggest that most people who carry out NPV analyses do so using cash flows taken straight from the descriptive part of the model. These, unfortunately, are often the wrong cash flows with which to calculate NPVs. Therefore, however theoretically correct the NPV measure may be, the decisions reached by applying it are often still wrong. The most common reasons for this are:

- including inappropriate cash flows and/or excluding appropiate ones
- failure to separate the investment decision (is this a good project?) from the financing decision (how can I raise the money to undertake the project?) and failure to correctly deal with their inter-relationship
- inconsistent treatment of inflation
- confusion over the number of years to model.

Appropriate cash flows

The cash flows that should be used for NPV analysis are often very different to those that appear in the descriptive part of the model, that is in the financial statements. As such, in order to define the cash flows on which to calculate NPV, it may be easiest to begin from scratch. The guiding rule for defining the cash flow for the NPV is that it should show a *complete* and *true* picture of the costs and benefits of the project to the firm. Four rules should be followed:

- cash flows, not profit figures, should be used
- 'sunk costs' should be ignored
- only costs arising as a direct result of the project should be included
- opportunity costs must be taken into account.

The need to use cash flow, not accounting profit, data in NPV has already been discussed. The reasons given were primarily to do with timing. For example, depreciation spreads out the cost of capital expenditure over many years, whereas discounting takes account of expenditure only when a cash flow occurs. The notion of accruals was given as another example of problems relating to timing.

NPV is a decision-making tool that is used to look into the future. Financial accounts are, by contrast, a means of reporting what has happened in the past. This difference means that the data required by NPV is not all available from accounts. Two key 'costs' that must be explicitly considered by NPV are sunk costs and opportunity costs.

Sunk costs are those that have already been incurred. They must be excluded from the NPV calculation because acceptance, or rejection, of a new project will not affect them. The example that follows illustrates this.

Example A firm of solicitors has been following a plan to expand their office network from Manchester into five surrounding towns and suburbs. At the start of the project they carried out an NPV evaluation and, as the NPV was positive, they went ahead. After a few offices had been opened, it was found that the venture was not proving as profitable as they originally anticipated. The partners in the practice have already invested a considerable sum in improving their administration to cope with the new offices. For example, new computers have been bought and software written. In addition, the firm has achieved BS 5750, based on a new organization structure designed to manage the proposed wide spread of offices. Although some of these costs could be recovered (for example by selling computers at a loss), most are *not* recoverable. What should the firm do? Should it continue with, halt or reverse its expansion programme?

The NPV approach to the problem is to carry out an analysis of what to do, ignoring the cost of the investment that has already taken place. For example, say that the initial investment in computer, administration and quality systems was £500 000 and that each branch office cost a further £75 000 in set-up costs, but that each office returned profits of £50 000 per annum, on average.

Carrying out an NPV analysis for all 5 branches, including the initial cost, produces a £72 687 NPV over 5 years at 10 per cent discount rate. However the two branches that have opened so far only give a total NPV of –£270 921. Opening a third branch will only increase this to –£156 382 (if the NPV calculation is carried out including the initial £500 000).

However, the £500 000 has been spent – it is a sunk cost. Opening a third branch actually produces an NPV of £114 539 on its own. The partners should, therefore, carry on – they cannot recover their initial investment, but they can make more profit to help alleviate the loss.

In a similar vein, the appraisal should not include any allocation of fixed costs. These will occur irrespective of whether or not the project goes ahead and are, therefore, irrelevant to the decision to proceed or not. If NPV is thought of as a means of making decisions, as opposed to a means of accounting or reporting, this conclusion will be easier to see.

NPV calculations should take account of opportunity costs. Opportunity cost can be defined as the amount of money foregone by taking one course of action instead of another. For example, if a pharmaceutical firm decides to focus its research and development effort on antiviral drugs, future sales of, say, beta-blockers may suffer as any technological lead may be lost. In this case, the calculation would have two parts: projected net increase in revenue from antiviral research and net reduction in revenue from beta-blockers.

Separation of investment and financing decisions

Most financial evaluation asks two questions, either implicitly or explicitly: first, 'Is this essentially a good investment?' and, second, 'Can it be financed?' One of the most common mistakes in calculating NPVs is to produce a set of cash flows that include both the project cash flows (such as revenues and operating costs) and financing costs. An NPV is then calculated on the net cash flow after both investment and financing elements have been taken into account. This is wrong. The NPV method implicitly assumes a cost of capital, that is the discount rate and, therefore, the majority of financing aspects of the project should be excluded from the NPV calculation.

Before going further, it is worth running through an example to show that simple financing really does not alter the NPV. As ever, though, there will be exceptions to this rule, some of which will be looked at below. Consider the following cash flow.

Table 2.2

		Period				
	0	1	2	3	4	NPV
Net Cash Flow (NCF)	– 400	200	200	50	100	
Discounted NCF (@10%)	–400	181.82	165.29	37.57	68.30	52.97

Now assume that, in order to finance the capital cost of 400, a loan is taken out, at a rate of 10 per cent interest, and is repayable over the four years of the project in 4 equal chunks. The loan schedule would look as follows.

Table 2.3

Period	0	1	2	3	4
B/f balance	0	400	300	200	100
Drawdown	400	–	–	–	–
Interest	–	40	30	20	10
Repayment	–	100	100	100	100
C/f balance	400	300	200	100	0

If the project's cash flow is added, together with the loan's cash flow, this yields the post-financing cash flow, as follows.

Table 2.4

Period	0	1	2	3	4
Net cash flow(NCF)	0 (–400+400)	60 (200–40–100)	70 (200–30–100)	–70 (50–20–100)	–10 (100–10–100)
Discounted NCF NCF	0	54.55	57.85	–52.59	–6.83

Summing the discounted cash flow gives an NPV, including financing, of 52.97 – exactly the same as before. If different loan repayment schedules are entered in place of four even payments, the result will be identical.

It also does not matter to the NPV calculation how the project was actually funded. If, for example, a mix of debt and equity had been used and the average cost of that mix was 10 per cent, then the analysis would have been identical. If a financial model is based on funding of this sort, there is no need to do anything more than decide on the appropriate discount rate (and, maybe, as we shall see later, to make some adjustments for inflation and risk).

In real life, financing structures are rarely going to be this simple. After all, the merchant banks make much of their money by constantly innovating complicated financial instruments. Happily, though, there is a way of dealing with non-standard financing side-effects as and when they arise. The technique will be illustrated by an example of the fees on a loan, as this is a common problem that is not dealt with by standard NPV analysis.

The methodology for incorporating financing side-effects into NPV was developed by an American financial economist, Stewart C. Myers, who in 1974, published a seminal article[3] in which he developed a technique called Adjusted Present Value (APV). APV is really a very straightforward idea. Essentially, it tells us first to calculate an NPV based on an assumption of all-equity financing. This is called the base case NPV. Then, making use of the fact that NPVs can be added together, APV proceeds by calculating mini-NPVs for each side-effect, such as different repayment methods and tax effects.

To take the example of loan fees, such as a commitment fee (which is a percentage levied on the loan left to draw) or an up-front arrangement fee, NPV does not take account of these and so their effect needs to be considered separately. The need to raise new equity to finance a project and, therefore, incur issue costs, is another financing cost that may need to be taken account of using APV.

In the case of issue costs or loan fees, the procedure is simply to calculate the NPV as normal, then deduct the present value of the fee. Thus, in the above example, if there was a 2 per cent fee for arranging the loan, the NPV of 52.97 would be reduced by 400×0.02, or 8, to 44.97. So, in this case, this side-effect does not alter the accept decision at all.

The tax effects of borrowing can also be incorporated using APV. Tax calculations will be looked at further in Chapter 5, but, very simply, corporation tax is levied at a certain rate – currently 33 per cent on taxable profits for large companies. Taxable profits, though, are not the same as accounting profits. The main difference is that, in place of accounting depreciation, there are a series of tax allowances. These allow certain capital expenditure (such as industrial buildings, plant and machinery and debt interest) to be deducted from profits before tax is calculated.

A project that will be partly or wholly financed by new debt therefore has a *potential* tax advantage over a project that is all-equity financed – 'potential' because tax is levied at a firm level and the firm as a whole must be generating sufficient taxable profits to make use of the tax relief on interest. If a firm believes that it can take advantage of tax relief on debt interest then an adjustment must be made to the NPV. This adjustment will be the PV of the interest payments multiplied by the tax rate.

Inflation

The question of whether or not to include the effects of inflation in the cash flows for the NPV calculation often cause modellers problems. Inflation cannot be ignored by any model, but there are different ways of taking it into account. It is this choice that gives rise to problems.

Before beginning the discussion, it is worth clarifying a couple of terms. There are two basic ways to treat inflation in a financial model:

- model cash flows in today's money terms, that is do not explicitly include the effects of inflation in cash flows. So, for example, if salary costs are £100 000 today, then, assuming constant output and efficiency, they would be modelled as £100 000 over each subsequent year; cash flows such as these are said to be in *real* terms
- model cash flows in money of the day, that is incorporating the effect of inflation, so, if salary costs are £100 000 today and inflation is expected to be 5 per cent per annum in perpetuity, salary costs would be modelled as £100 000(1.05) next year, £100 000(1.05)² the year after and so on; these cash flows are said to be in *nominal* terms.

These terms cause great confusion, and this is heightened because cash flows cannot be considered on their own – the discount rate comes into the equation as well. To illustrate this, consider the following, real, cash flow.

Table 2.5

t = 0	t = 1	t = 2	t = 3	t = 4	t = 5
−150	−10	30	98	140	− 50

Assume that the interest rate quoted in today's paper is 12 per cent. Discounting at this rate gives an NPV of –4.66. Now, if inflation of 5 per cent per annum is assumed, the cash flow would look as follows, expressed in nominal terms.

Table 2.6

t = 0	t = 1	t = 2	t = 3	t = 4	t = 5
−150	−10.50	33.08	113.45	170.17	−63.81

If this cash flow were to be discounted at the same rate, that is 12 per cent, the NPV would be 19.69. Therefore, according to these results, if real cash flows are used the project should be rejected and if nominal are used it should be accepted. Despite the fact that this conclusion is often seen in practice, it is entirely wrong. The reason it is wrong is because a *nominal* discount rate was used to discount a *real* cash flow. The simple rule to follow is to discount a *nominal* cash flow with a *nominal* discount rate and to discount a *real* cash flow with a *real* interest rate. There is a simple equation for deriving the real interest rate:

$$\text{Real rate} = \frac{1 + \text{Nominal rate}}{1 + \text{Inflation rate}} - 1$$

If the real discount rate, of 6.67 per cent in this case, is used to discount the real cash flow, the NPV is 19.69 – identical to using the nominal rate to discount the nominal cash flow.

On balance, it will normally be least confusing to work in nominal terms, that is, using the market rates of interest and incorporating inflation into the cash flows. There are a number of reasons for this. First, if cash flows are not inflated, the total amount of financing that will be required cannot be predicted. For example, if the capital expenditure for a project is spread over, say, three years, it is likely that inflation will occur before all expenditure has been undertaken and, consequently, more funding will be required. Knowing the total funding requirement is important if outside funding is to be used as the amount of the facility available will be set at the beginning of the project. Banks will be highly reluctant to increase this later on, and they will expect a commitment fee for making the money available in between times. The same argument can be applied to working capital. The second reason for working in nominal terms is that it allows differentials between revenues and costs and between different categories of costs to be easily modelled. Therefore, if pay is expected to rise faster than raw materials, this can be taken into account. Even if inflation is not modelled in full it is still probably prudent to consider these differential effects. The third reason for working with nominal cash flows is that tax will be calculated based on them.

Period of analysis

DCF analysis is used widely, in situations as diverse as cost–benefit analysis for new public works projects, corporate planning and joint venture structuring. However, its roots and largest user base lie in capital budgeting, looking at such problems as whether or not to purchase a new machine or build a new factory. In capital budgeting analyses, the period of time over which the analysis should be carried out is generally known. For example, the specification for a machine may state that its life is expected to be ten years. In other areas, such as corporate planning, the period of analysis may not be fixed by physical characteristics, but there is likely to be an established 'planning horizon' that may be taken as the period to use. In some cases, though, it may be quite difficult to decide how many years to project forward.

If there is no 'natural' length of the project to take, then one must be derived. The choice of period over which NPV is calculated can affect the result radically. It is important, therefore, to make a sensible choice. In considering this, three issues are worth bearing in mind:

- the certainty that can be attributed to cash flow projections normally declines dramatically with distance into the future
- discounting makes future cash flows less important
- as the discount rate rises, future cash flows become much less important.

The following figures illustrate this by showing the present value of £100 at 10 per cent and 20 per cent discount rate over 5, 10, 15 and 20 years.

Table 2.7

Period	0	5	10	15	20
PV @ 10%	£100	£62.09	£38.55	£23.94	£14.86
PV @ 20%	£100	£40.19	£16.15	£6.49	£2.61

It is possible to carry on the cash flows at some steady state of growth after the period when good information runs out. However, it is sometimes rather tempting to use this method in order to boost the NPV of projects, which in reality will run out of competitive advantage, and, hence, positive cash flows, long before this far-off point in the growth formula calculations is reached.

SETTING THE DISCOUNT RATE

Introduction

Up to now, it has been assumed that the discount rate is equivalent to the bank interest rate or some equivalent measure, such as the return on government Gilts. The rationale behind this assumption was that this rate could be considered to be the return that would be available to the organization if the project was not undertaken. There are three reasons why that assumption is an oversimplification.

First, there is almost always a differential between lending and borrowing rates. Therefore, if the bank lending rate of, say, 10 per cent is used to discount a project, but the money to finance it actually costs 14 per cent, there is a danger that projects could be accepted that do not generate sufficient return to cover their cost of capital.

Second, there is no one interest rate – loans made with different repayment periods will have different interest rates. This difference is known as the term structure of interest rates[4].

Third, if a project is accepted at a discount rate that is lower than the return currently being received by shareholders from their investment in the business, their return will be diluted and, hence, the value of the company will fall. To put it another way, if it is assumed that the share price is equal to the discounted sum of the expected future dividends that will accrue to that share, then the IRR of that flow (which can be assumed to carry on indefinitely) will represent the expected return on equity. If a project is undertaken that has an IRR lower than that, then the expected dividend stream will reduce, so reducing the value of the share price and, hence, the value of the company.

The discount rate that should be used, therefore, is the cost of capital. Using the cost of capital as the discount rate means that only projects offering returns greater than their financing costs will be accepted. As the cost of capital also reflects the return to providers of capital, it will ensure that only opportunities increasing the value of the firm go ahead.

So, how is the cost of capital to be calculated? The answer is, unfortunately, rather fraught, but it is crucial to the success of any financial appraisal. Nevertheless, when struggling with the problem in practice, it is important not to become bogged down in the technicalities of setting the discount rate at the expense of ensuring that the cash flow forecasts to be discounted are sound.

Estimating the cost of capital

Businesses are normally financed by some mix of debt and equity. In the case of large companies the mix might actually be highly complicated, but in its simplest form it can be no more than the savings of the owner and an overdraft from the local bank. Debt capital will typically have a lower cost (as expressed by its interest rate) than equity. This reflects the fact that debt interest will be paid before dividends to equity.

Cost of equity

The cost of debt is normally fairly easy to estimate, it is the interest rate. The cost of equity is more complicated and it is the estimation of this cost that causes most of the problems in arriving at a discount rate. In the discussion above, a model in which equity value was related to the discounted expected future dividend value was introduced. More formally this can be stated as:

$$V_e = \sum_{t=1}^{\infty} \frac{D_t}{(1 + CoE)^t}$$

where V_e is the value of equity, D_t is the expected dividend in period t and CoE is the cost of equity.

Ignoring risk for now, the major problem with this formula is in estimating the values of D_t in perpetuity. One means of doing this is to assume that dividends will grow at a certain rate – g – for ever. A useful formula for this is known as the 'Gordon Model' of a growing perpetuity.[5] The formula for the PV of a growing perpetuity is:

$$PV(D) = \frac{D}{i - g}$$

where D is the dividend now, i is the discount rate and g the growth rate.

If the Gordon Model is substituted in the value of equity formula, the result is:

$$CoE = \frac{D_0(1 + g)}{SP} + g$$

where SP is the ex dividend share price and the other terms are as before.

To take an example, assume that this year's dividend was 23p per share and that the share price is 306p ex dividend. Dividend growth has averaged 4 per cent per annum over the last 5 years and this growth is expected to continue. Therefore:

$$CoE = \frac{23(1.04)}{306} + 0.04$$

$$= 11.82 \text{ per cent}$$

This is now a reasonable working model with which to estimate the cost of equity. As companies often like to maintain a steady growth in dividends, the value of g can often be reasonably estimated from past data.

The failings of the dividend growth rate model lie mainly with its treatment of risk. If this model is to be used to calculate the cost of capital for use in an NPV calculation, there is an implicit assumption that the risk[6] of the project is the same as the general level of risk currently faced by the equity holders in their investment in the firm. For example, if a high street food retailer was evaluating a project to buy a chain of high street food stores, then the assumption of the risks being the same would, presumably, hold. If, however, the same retailer was evaluating a project to buy a banana importer, then that project would alter the risk profile faced by the equity holders. The equity valuation model would therefore not provide the correct cost of equity figure. Methods of dealing with situations like this are discussed below.

Overall cost of capital

Now that we have estimated the cost of equity and we know the cost of debt from the interest rate, some composite rate is required that can be taken as the overall cost of capital to use as the discount rate in the NPV calculations. The most straightforward way of doing this is to calculate the weighted average cost of capital, commonly referred to as the WACC. WACC is simply an average of the costs of equity and debt weighted according to their relative proportions in the capital structure. The proportions are determined from *market values*. Take the following example.

Shares outstanding	2.3m
Ex dividend share price	56p
Dividend yield	5.1 per cent
Historic growth rate in dividend	4.5 per cent per annum
Total debt outstanding	£427 000
Average interest on debt	7.81 per cent

$$\text{CoE} = \frac{(56 \times 0.051)1.045}{56} + 0.045$$

$$= 9.83\%$$

$$
\begin{aligned}
\text{Market value of debt and equity} &= 2.3\text{m} \times £0.56 + £427\ 000 \\
&= £1.288\text{m} + £0.427\text{m} \\
&= £1.715\text{m}
\end{aligned}
$$

$$\text{WACC} = \frac{1.288}{1.715} \times 9.83\% + \frac{0.427}{1.715} \times 7.81\%$$

$$= 9.33\%$$

In real life, the calculation would probably be more complicated as companies are financed by a wide variety of types of finance. The principle would, however, remain the same – to weight each cost of finance by its market value. Unfortunately, although the WACC method is reasonably easy to apply, its use is limited because of the considerations of risk referred to above. In theory, WACC should *only* be used to derive the cost of capital if the project is very small in relation to the firm as a whole and so will not alter the gearing, or risk profile, of the company. In reality, its use will be acceptable in many cases, if only to provide a first pass discount rate. Another method, which has fewer theoretical problems, and can deal with risk better is examined next.

RISK

Types of risk

DCF analysis is concerned with looking into the future to assess the expected returns on a project. By definition, therefore, the process involves making estimates and using judgement. These judgements may turn out to be correct, but more than likely will not because the returns will be subject to a myriad of complicated processes, each themselves subject to chance and uncertainty. Therefore, the best that the financial modeller can hope to do is assess the likely extent of the risk facing a project and consider whether the return offered is sufficient to compensate for that risk.

Although risk has not yet been directly addressed, the analysis of the WACC implied it. If there were no risk, then both debt and equity would require the same rates of return. The premium that equity commands is to compensate the equity providers for the risk that there will be insufficient cash flow to pay a dividend or that, in the event of liquidation, the claims of debt providers equal or exceed the amount of cash realized.

Any investment – whether through debt or equity – in a commercial company is subject to risk because there is always the possibility that the company will become bankrupt. The required return on corporate investment can, therefore, be thought of as some risk-free rate (for example, the return from buying government bonds, such as Gilts), plus a premium for commercial risk. As the risk on equity is higher than on debt, the risk premium, and hence the return required by equity, will be higher than that of debt.

Investors have a number of choices open to them in deciding what to do with their money. The first choice is whether to provide debt or equity capital. The second is where to invest it – in which industry, in a large or small firm, new start-up, buy-out, buy-in, recovery or expansion and so on. The risk of the investment will vary quite markedly with the choice made. However, most professional investors aim to build a portfolio of investments to diversify, or spread, their risks. In its simplest form the objective of diversification is to try and ensure that all the eggs are not in one basket. The way in which diversification works is fundamental to evaluating risk in financial modelling.

The basis of diversification is that the risk associated with each investment can be split into two parts: the risk specific to the investment, arising from factors peculiar to that investment, and non-specific risk from general market and macro-economic factors. Specific risk is also known as unsystematic or diversifiable risk, and non-specific risk is also known as systematic, non-diversifiable or market risk.

Using the capital asset pricing model to handle risk

Observation of the real economy (as distinct from the capital markets) in terms of measures such as profitability and bankruptcy shows that different industries respond to economic conditions in quite different ways. For example, the construction industry is very sensitive to fluctuations in the economic cycle, so, in boom times, new houses, shops and offices are built, while in recession they are not. Food retailing and brewing are examples of industries that are less affected by the economic cycle.

The way in which the return on an investment[7] moves in relation to changes in the real economy measures the degree of non-specific risk to which investment is subjected. The measure of this risk is called beta (ß). More precisely, an investment's beta measures the degree of correlation between movements in its price and that of the market[8]. A share's beta can, for example, be derived from a simple time series regression of movements in the market index (such as the FT-SE All Share Index) against movements in the share's price. This is shown in Figure 2.1. Alternatively, estimates of beta can be obtained on subscription from agencies such as the London Business School's Risk Management Service.

Beta is important because it measures the part of the risk that investors cannot diversify away by building a portfolio of shares. If it is assumed that investors are rational and risk-averse, it may reasonably be concluded that they will always seek to diversify away the risk that they can (that is, the specific risk) through a portfolio. Therefore, for the purposes of deciding on the risk premium that investors will seek, only non-specific risk, as measured by beta, will matter.

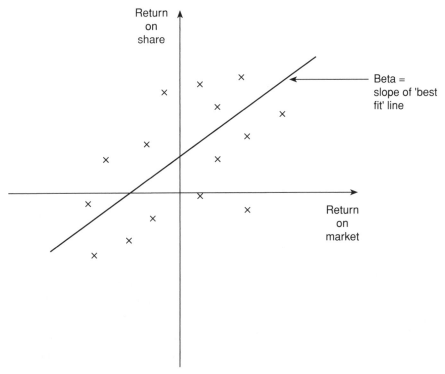

Figure 2.1 The derivation of beta

An important theory, called the capital asset pricing model (CAPM), states that the risk premium investors will seek on an investment is directly proportional to the beta of the investment. Although the CAPM was developed under a whole series of highly unrealistic assumptions, it does appear to describe the real world fairly reasonably and, as such, it is quite widely used. The formula can be stated as:

$$E(R)_{sharej} = \text{RF} + \beta(E(R)_{market} - \text{RF})$$

where $E(R)$ is the expected return and RF is the risk-free rate of interest. Note that care should be taken to use an interest rate appropriate to the length of the project, that is base long-term RF rates on long-term interest rates. It is estimated that the average risk premium $(E(R)_{market} - \text{RF})$ has, historically, averaged around 9 per cent in the UK.

This formula provides an alternative to the dividend valuation model for estimating the required return on equity. CAPM has the advantage that it is based on observable market prices. Therefore, so long as betas are relatively constant over time (which various studies have suggested that they are – at least at sector level), CAPM offers a useful risk-adjusted approach. CAPM also has the significant advantage that it can cope with changes in gearing.

In order to apply CAPM to non-traded investments, an appropriate beta must be derived that reflects the level of non-specific risk and gearing structure of the project. The starting point for this is to decide on the most comparable shares to use in order to find a proxy of beta for the project. In deciding the shares to use, it is the non-specific risk of the project that should be the criterion. For example, if a consumer electronics manufacturer is considering buying an electronics retailer, the appropriate betas to look at would be consumer electronics retailing, not manufacturing. A sector average, rather than an individual company's beta, should be used in this case as the investment will not be in the individual share.

Once a suitable beta has been set, it must be adjusted to take account of any difference in the gearing between the project and the sector chosen. This is because gearing will alter the volatility of the investment with respect to the market. For example, a highly geared firm is more likely to become bankrupt during a recession than the equivalent low-geared firm. An example will illustrate this.

Example (Note that the beta and gearing figures are fictitious). A leading publisher is considering purchasing a regional chain of bookshops. The beta of the publisher is 1.34, against an average for the sector of 1.22. The bookshops are a privately owned firm and so have no beta of their own available. The beta of their sector is 0.85. The publisher has gearing (defined as the ratio of the *market value* of debt to total *market value* of the firm) of 43 per cent against a sector average of 36 per cent. The bookshops have gearing of 55 per cent, against a sector average of 41 per cent. The acquisition is to be financed by a combination of a rights issue and issue of loan notes. The effect of this will be to change the publisher's gearing to 49 per cent. The risk-free rate, as represented by the 5-year interest rate, is 8.2 per cent. The risk premium of the equity market is assumed to be 9 per cent. What cost of equity capital should be used?

The first issue is which beta to use. As the objective is to assess the non-specific risk of the proposed investment (and that investment is in a different sector to the publisher), the beta of the publisher and the publishing sector is not relevant. In this case, as there is no beta for the target firm available, the beta of the sector should be used. The bookshop sector beta – 0.85 – has an assumption of gearing implicit in it – in this case, 36 per cent. However, the financial risk for the equity investment will be determined by the gearing of the publisher *post-acquisition,* that is 49 per cent. The implicit gearing in the beta must, therefore, be removed and the appropriate gearing put in its place. The way to do this is as follows:

$$\text{Ungeared beta} = \beta_{sector} \times (1\text{-Gearing}_{sector})$$
$$= 0.85 \times (1\text{-}0.36)$$
$$= 0.54$$

$$\text{Regeared beta} = \text{Ungeared } \beta \times [1/(1\text{-Gearing}_{project})]$$
$$= 0.54 \times [1/(1\text{-}0.49)]$$
$$= 1.06$$

CAPM can now be used to find the cost of equity capital:

$$\text{CoE} = 8.2\% + 1.06 \times 9 \text{ per cent}$$
$$= 17.7 \text{ per cent}$$

The figure derived from the CAPM can now be used as the discount rate in a WACC calculation. If APV were being used, the beta would not need to be regeared as it is assumed that the base case is all-equity financed.

Despite the apparently scientific calculation we have just witnessed, caution is required in using the cost of equity figure derived. This is because the sector beta that was used as the basis for deciding on the project beta is problematical:

- it is only an estimate from a regression line and, therefore, subject to a margin of error
- the effect that tax relief on interest has in reducing the effective cost of debt has been ignored
- beta is affected not only by sensitivity to the economic cycle and the level of gearing for which an adjustment was made, but also by other factors, such as the sector's ratio of fixed to total costs
- the return on shares, with which beta is estimated, implicitly includes the market's estimation of the share's growth potential, which may be different to the project's.

It is possible to make further adjustments to beta to compensate for these problems, but any such adjustments are in themselves estimates, so the question must be asked as to whether or not it is worth taking the analysis further. Many managers would argue that, in the majority of cases, it is not.

Another approach to handling risk

CAPM works by adjusting the discount rate to take account of risk. An alternative approach is to alter the cash flows themselves. Although this approach will not distinguish between specific and non-specific risk as neatly as CAPM and is, therefore, less theoretically 'pure', it may be a preferable approach in practice because:

- it avoids the intricacies of estimating beta
- it focuses managers' attention on the topic for which their practical business knowledge can be of most use, that is, the cash flows.

There are two main ways of adjusting the cash flows:

- replace fixed estimates of cash flows with probability functions to produce an expected NPV (ENPV); this is called *probability analysis*
- run a variety of different scenarios (such as varying revenue ± 25 per cent) to discover how the NPV responds to changes in key variables; this is called *sensitivity analysis.*

The problems with sensitivity analysis were discussed in Chapter 1 and, although it is by far the most common approach to risk management in practice, it cannot really be considered a true risk management tool. All sensitivity analysis will do is say that if a certain outcome happens, the result is expected to be y. Its wide use appears to stem not from its inherent usefulness, but from the fact that it avoids the difficult problem of examining the likelihood of various outcomes *actually* occurring.

Probability analysis works from the premise that many cash flows are unknown. Takes sales, for example. A firm might expect sales of £500 000 for a new product. This might have been guestimated by salesmen, forecasted using econometric analysis by planners or been estimated as a result of market research by marketers. In each case, though, it may or may not happen. Probability analysis asks how likely it, or a number of alternative possible outcomes, are to happen. A simple example illustrates the principle.

EXAMPLE Assume that the revenue of a new product may be only £400, £500, or £600 in its first year. The fixed costs will be £300 and the variable costs may be 15, 30 or 45 per cent of revenues. The possible outcomes (that is, the profits) are shown over.

Table 2.8

	Revenue		
Variable costs	£400	£500	£600
15%	£40	£125	£210
30%	(£20)	£50	£120
45%	(£80)	(£25)	£30

Sensitivity analysis concludes that, if the worst, comes to the worst, the firm could lose £80, but it could also gain £210 if all goes well. Not a great deal of help. As a first pass at improving on that analysis, assume that all nine outcomes are equally likely. What profit could we most likely expect in this case?

The answer is simply an average of the possible outcomes, that is, £50 – an advance on sensitivity analysis, even without additional information. However, now assume that the firm can make a better guess of the probability of different outcomes (as it almost certainly could). The probabilities of each event are estimated as follows:

Table 2.9

Revenue	Probability
£400	30%
£500	50%
£600	20%

Table 2.10

Variable cost	Probability
15%	15%
30%	70%
45%	15%

Assuming that the outcome of revenue does not affect the outcome of variable cost, then the expected profit is the average of the profit figures given above, weighted by the probabilities, that is:

$$(30\% \times 15\% \times £40) + (30\% \times 70\% \times -£20) + ... = £4.78$$

Not quite such a good result!

Fairly clearly, this type of analysis can be extended to multiperiod cash flows and an ENPV produced. However, the above example was very simple – a small number of possible states, each of which was known. Real life is not like that – sales could be just about anything, from zero to the capacity level of the firm. There will also be many variables interacting together – many sources of revenue, many costs, different possible working capital scenarios and so on.

The solution lies in software that allows variables in a spreadsheet to be specified, not as discrete points (say, £500), but as probability functions, such as 'normally distributed around a mean of £500 with a standard deviation of £50'. Once the model is built, the software will run a large number of iterations and build up a table of ENPVs. This distribution may then be viewed graphically.

Further reading

This chapter has had to skim many complicated topics. The following books all provide further discussion (the last book is slightly more advanced than the others).

Brealey, R.A., and Myers, S.C., *Principles of Corporate Finance*, fourth edition
Ross, S.A., Westerfield, R.W. and Jaffe, J.F. *Corporate Finance*, second edition
Lumby, S., *Investment Appraisal and Financing Decisions*, fourth edition
Ivison, S., Moss, C., and Simpson M., (editors), *British Readings in Financial Management*

Notes

[1] Three years' compound interest, that is £350 000 × (1.08)^3 = £440 899.20.

[2] Sometimes IRR is also called the yield, the marginal efficiency of investment (MEI) or the marginal efficiency of capital (MEC). The term MEC is often used in economics texts as the MEC was initially popularized by the economist J.M. Keynes.

[3] S.C. Myers 'Interactions Corporate Financing and Investment Decisions – Implications for capital Budgeting', Journal of Finance, vol. 29, March 1974, pp.1–25.

[4] For an introduction to why short and long-term interest rates vary, see Brealy and Myers, *Principles of Corporate Finance*, fourth edition, Chapter 23.

[5] A perpetuity is stream of identical cash flows extending for ever.

[6] More correctly, the 'systematic risk' of the project. This is examined more fully under Risk later in this chapter.

[7] The investments discussed here are, by implication, tradable investments (as they have a market price), most commonly shares. The discussion will later be broadened out to show how the estimation of risk on tradable investments can be applied to assess risk on non-tradable investments, such as new ventures and capital investments.

[8] More formally: $\beta_x = \dfrac{\sigma_{xm}}{\sigma^2_m}$ where σ_{xm} is the covariance between the return on share x and the market return, and σ^2_m is the variance of the return on the market.

Part II

MODEL PLANNING AND DESIGN

3

MODEL PLANNING

INTRODUCTION

Of the hundreds of thousands of financial models in use, it would be interesting to know how many have been systematically thought through before someone sat down in front of a screen and started programming the computer. The size and importance of the model will clearly have some bearing on the amount of forethought given. It would, for example, be more likely for a major strategic planning model to be planned out in advance than would the cash forecast for a corner shop.

Whether or not the model was planned will also have been affected by the software medium used. For example, modelling packages that build models using traditional programming techniques, such as FCS, are very difficult to use without preplanning, whereas spreadsheets positively encourage trial and error. This is because in the programming approach data, relationships (such as profit = sales – costs) and reports must all be defined separately. In a spreadsheet, a single cell is both either data or relationship and the output in one; the only additional effort required is to press the print key.

So, what is meant by planning a model and why should it be a good thing to do? In many ways, the answers to these two questions are related. To answer them, it is necessary to think about *why* a financial model is built in the first place. It is built to answer some question or to illuminate a problem more clearly. A typical question might be to examine the business impacts of a number of different strategic options. The answer to this question is important to the planning manager asking it and, therefore, the manager will be concerned to get the most insightful or accurate result possible. This result will only fulfil the need if the model:

- provides a greater insight into the issue than is possible using other techniques
- is arithmetically correct, that is, it adds up
- is logically correct, that is, the relationships within the model accurately

reflect the underlying business processes being modelled. For example, if the model calculates the firm's market share by comparing its price with competitors' prices, then, for the model to be logically correct, that relationship should be observable in practice.

Planning a model is the first step in making sure a model will meet the business objectives asked of it. Model planning, therefore, divides into two phases when the following questions are asked.

- Should a model be built and is it the correct approach?
- If it is, then how should it be built so as to ensure its accuracy?

REASONS MODELS ARE NOT PLANNED

That a model should be planned in the way outlined above is common sense. Experience suggests, though, that common sense somehow disappears when it comes to the crunch and modellers still launch headlong into programming. This seems to be because, although planning models before starting is commonly thought of as a 'good thing', rather like documenting models, it is something that model builders tend not to like doing. There are many ways in which this dislike is rationalized to produce reasons for there *not* being a need to plan models. These reasons need to be recognized as being misleading. Some of the most common arguments, together with commentary, are given below.

- *Argument* Models are usually under pressure to show results as quickly as possible. It is often rather difficult for a modeller (who is often one of the more junior members of a team) to turn around to his or her boss, who often does not recognize the complexities involved, and say, 'Sorry, but before I can answer that question I shall have to plan out my model'.
  Comment An important precondition for effective model building is that model builders and users communicate more effectively. This point is discussed further below.
- *Argument* It is commonly believed that spreadsheet models do not need to be planned – their flexibility means that the structure of a model can be changed easily and problems fixed.
  Comment This is an appealing argument, but while spreadsheets *do* allow changes to be easily made, their lack of an imposed structure means that problems are more likely to occur because all relationships and paths in the model must be defined from scratch.

- *Argument* Most models are simple and, therefore, planning is an unnecessary and bureaucratic overhead.
  Comment Financial models often begin life as small and straightforward. However, models typically expand dramatically from their initial scope. The reasons for this appear to be a combination of the ease with which spreadsheets allow changes to be made and frustration with the value added by simple models containing only accounting tautologies.
- *Argument* When the need for a financial model is first identified, its precise objectives cannot be specified because external events continually change the requirement. However, because development times are so long, modelling is better started sooner rather than later.
  Comment This argument can be addressed in a number of ways, but there is no doubt that the problem is very real in practice as most financial modelling is concerned with examining future uncertainties. While it is not possible to eliminate that uncertainty, it can be reduced by a combination of thorough preplanning and structuring the model in such a way that changes can be incorporated more easily (this second issue is examined more closely in Chapters 5 and 7).

It is not just modellers, overly keen on getting stuck in, who perpetuate these fallacies, but also users of models who have the wrong expectations of the effort – output relationship involved in financial modelling. Both these groups contribute to poor planning. The arguments above mainly relate to the technical reasons for models being planned, but there are also a number of sound business reasons for planning:

- financial models are often used to make critical business decisions, so they need to be correct and models that are planned stand a much greater chance of being accurate than those that are not
- a large majority of financial models have a significant number of errors and, although in some cases these arise from poor technical design of the model or from lack of knowledge among modellers, a significant contributory factor is haphazard model development caused by poor planning
- planning reduces overdependence on one or two individuals holding all knowledge about the model in their heads and enables the development workload for large models to be split among a number of people rather than be handled by one modeller
- spreadsheets – on which most financial modelling takes place – are inherently unstructured and, therefore, require control to be imposed on them if errors are to be avoided.

A number of good reasons to plan models. However, models do vary in size and importance. The challenge is to bring an element of structure to the modelling process without creating a bureaucratic monster.

PRE-CONDITIONS FOR EFFECTIVE PLANNING

It is difficult to argue that planning models is anything other than a good idea and will almost certainly improve their eventual quality. However, there is a considerable distance between accepting the proplanning arguments and actually planning each and every model. Part of the reason planning is often not done is that it is perceived as being boring, but another part is the lack of what might be called 'a planning culture' within the financial modelling world. Many factors contribute to this, some of which were discussed in Chapter 1. There are, however, two positive steps that can be taken to facilitate effective model planning, looked at below.

Step 1: change attitudes to modelling

Typically, different individuals are involved in using, as opposed to building/running, financial models. The modellers (people who build and run models) tend to be younger than and junior to the users. There are a number of reasons for this. Younger people often being more PC-literate, people progress from 'doing' to 'managing' as they get older and move up the corporate ladder and as a result of the idea of effective resource allocation – modelling takes a lot of time and therefore it can be an inefficient and expensive use of resources to have an experienced manager building models. Financial modelling is also often seen as good training as it provides an overview of the business and how it works.

This distinction between roles, however sensible, inevitably results in some loss of communication. Users may not articulate their requirements sufficiently clearly – possibly because they do not fully understand the complexities and intricacies of the model. Conversely, the modeller might not have sufficient business knowledge to translate the user's ideas into a model. The differences in grade and standing will also contribute to the problems. A keen young modeller will often make rash promises and tell the boss 'not to worry – that is no problem', when perhaps he or she does not fully understand all the issues or has not grasped the complexities of the situation to be modelled.

The arguments for distinguishing between the user and modeller roles are persuasive, but what needs to be changed is the attitude that the roles need to be so hierarchical and divorced from each other as is often the case today.

Users must be prepared to invest time with modellers in agreeing the purpose and goal of the model and in setting clear performance targets for the modeller in the form of milestones. Modellers must be brought into the process they are modelling. This means that junior modellers should at least sit in on key meetings and more experienced modellers should be seen as part of the team involved in negotiating a new deal, implementing closures or whatever the model is concerned with. A modeller who does nothing but sit in front of a PC all day every day is either the wrong person for the job or, more likely, a poorly utilized resource.

Step 2: internalize planning into the quality culture

Many organizations have implemented total quality management (TQM) and ISO 9000/BS 5750 Quality systems. Many more aspire to these standards. An essential part of both TQM and ISO 9000/BS 5750 is the notion of getting it right first time. If a financial model is not thought through before it is begun, it is highly *unlikely* to get it right first time or even second or third time. Too often, financial models seem to be left outside the Quality system. The reasons for this are not entirely clear, but they include the common perception of financial models as essentially *ad hoc* fixes that are short-lived and, therefore, somehow not as important, in the quality sense, as, say, the financial and operations systems. When it is considered that some of the largest projects in the world (such as the Channel Tunnel) stand or fall by the results of a financial model, this is clearly difficult to justify.

This is not to say that some organizations have not taken steps to improve the quality of financial models. However, the approach adopted has been essentially historic, such as auditing the model once it has been completed and/or a post-project review. The question remains as to how to ensure that a premodelling plan is formulated, without creating too much red tape. In the next section, an approach to model planning that is broadly compatible with Quality management is presented.

EVALUATING THE BUSINESS CASE

The first stage in any financial modelling exercise should be some consideration of what the business objectives to be met are and whether building a financial model is the best way to meet them. The reason for stressing this is that building a financial model is often a kind of gut reaction for managers: printouts of cash flows often seem to give comfort of a sort not found in written reports.

The decision as to whether or not to use a financial model should be based on four prior steps:

- definition of business goals
- analysis of how a financial model can contribute towards these goals
- evaluation of alternative options
- assessment of modelling risk.

Clearly the size and complexity of the proposed model will affect how these evaluations are made, but some standardized approach it generally desirable because it will help ensure that similar criteria are applied to *all* modelling decisions. One method of achieving consistency is to have a standard procedure for approving model proposals. This might consist of one or more preprinted forms or it could be a set of points to be considered in a written or verbal report (an example is given in the Appendix to this chapter).

Definition of business goals

The business goal is quite simply the business issue being examined and that which the proposed model is supposed to help evaluate. To say that a model should be built for some sensible reason seems blindingly obvious. It is, but many models are created and expanded without proper consideration having ever been given to the question of why they are needed in the first place. There are two main implications of this.

The first is that models built without a clearly defined purpose will take longer to develop, because they require frequent rewrites to resolve misunderstandings between modeller and sponsor. The second is that models may be built where financial modelling provides either an incomplete or the wrong approach to answering the desired question.

Specifying the purpose of a model is a matter of briefly stating the business problem that the model is to address, that is, what output is required. For example, a model of intercompany transfer pricing might be created by one part of the firm for the purpose of:

- understanding the current structure of costing and charging within the company and identifying the size and nature of the charges to the business arising from other management areas
- using this understanding to negotiate changes to current cost allocations and recharging mechanisms
- examining the impact of future events, such as the proposed reorganization, on costs.

The contribution of the model to goals

Having established the business goal, the next step is to consider how a financial model can meet the goal. Needless to say, like all techniques, financial models are good at some things and bad at others. It follows, therefore, that they should only be used for what they are good at. The sorts of application to which financial models are suited tend to be those where there is good data availability and the complexity of the situation is limited. For example financial models are good at:

- summarizing existing information, such as multidivision consolidation
- extrapolating current data forward using the simpler statistical techniques, such as exponential smoothing and basic regression analysis (see Chapter 4)
- transforming engineering-type specifications into financial forecasts, for example, a machine may have a known maintenance programme related to usage and time, efficiency related to throughput and so on, so, if a demand forecast is input into this specification, the machine's cost function is easily built up
- evaluating different financial structures for a given project cash flow
- automating large numbers of routine calculations, such as in assessing the IRR of a capital project.

Financial models tend to fall down in situations where:

- there is fuzziness in relationships, for example when demand cannot be described in one easy equation
- the evaluation is concerned with concepts, rather than hard facts
- there is a gap in understanding – financial modelling is basically a means of analysing existing knowledge (most commonly when that knowledge is expressed in numerical terms), it cannot then create new knowledge, although it can certainly improve the understanding of, and interpretation of, existing knowledge
- base data is incomplete – financial models often need vast quantities of data to drive them, indeed, the data requirement of a model increases much more rapidly than does the complexity of the model, for example, in a model to examine a company reorganization, not only the direct cost impacts of closing certain functions must be known, but also the impact on the activity and, therefore, the cost of other associated functions.

Evaluating non-modelling approaches

The problem with managers turning to financial models as a gut reaction is a difficult one to overcome. In some cases, building a financial model will be the right approach, but, in others, some alternative approach might yield better results. Any model proposal must address this issue by considering how a number of alternative methods might be used in place of modelling and how they compare with the modelling solution. The consideration of alternatives will be particularly important in the case of large models that might consume significant resources.

In considering non-modelling options, the plan must first review whether the stated purpose of the model implies using existing knowledge and analysing quantitative information. If there are no elements of this, then clearly modelling is entirely the wrong option. However, if, as is more likely, there are some elements of quantitative analysis and some of needing new information and resolving qualitative issues, then the task becomes how to decide where to use modelling, where to use other techniques and how best to integrate the output from each study.

So, what other approaches are available apart from financial modelling? In the case of gaining new knowledge, some form of research is the main approach. This might be, for example, market research of customer buying habits, it might be a statistical study of cost patterns or it might be establishing the types and conditions of financial instruments available. Each of these pieces of research generate knowledge in that they provide information to the analysis that was not previously known by that process. In many cases, once that knowledge has been assimilated, it can be analysed by means of a financial model.

If a greater degree of qualitative analysis is required, tools such as management workshops or seminars led by a facilitator, brainstorming and task forces reporting on specific issues may provide a more productive route than financial modelling. They also provide a means of sharing existing knowledge and, therefore, potentially also introducing new knowledge to the modelling process.

Assessing the modelling risk

The next step in planning financial models is to recognize and plan for risk. Some models are very much more difficult to complete than others. For example, a model of a new project that simply inputs revenue projections from a market research report, is likely to be easier than a model that attempts to model the effects of competition on demand. One of the main problems with financial modelling is that models run over time because the complexity of what they are trying to achieve has been underestimated. It is essential, therefore, to try to gauge this in advance so that a decision can be made as to how best to proceed, for example in using more experienced modellers or outside consultancy support.

High-risk factors

The risk for any model plan can be thought of as the likelihood of *not* delivering the specified model on time and to budget. Because there is such a wide range of models that may be created, it is not possible to say, for example, that a model of type x will take 3.5 days to complete. What can be done is to identify a number of high-risk factors (routines that are potentially difficult and time consuming) that provide a warning that, if included in a model, it can be expected to take longer to complete and may give rise to difficulties.

High-risk features include:

- multicurrency operation
- modelling competitive responses
- large numbers of cost–revenue interrelationships
- goal seeking, such as targeting a specific gearing level
- multiple sources of finance
- modelling of risk
- multiple tax regimes.

Features that introduce lower levels risks of but are still time consuming include:

- complicated treatment of tax, such as ACT and group relief in the UK
- working in 'real' terms (that is, with cash flows that exclude inflation, but with a discount rate adjusted for inflation).

As an approximate guide, any model that contains a high-risk feature is likely to take several days longer than the same model without these features are included to complete. The risk level when multiple high-risk features can be thought of as very broadly multiplicative. This means that a high number of these high-risk features can quite easily cripple a model's development.

The implications of risk

There are three main implications of the risk assessment. First, models that have high-risk factors present in them should be developed by experienced staff who have the necessary knowledge. In some cases, additional advice will still need to be sought on specialist issues such as treatment of overseas tax. The second implication is that complicated models may be very expensive in terms of time and resources. Therefore, the value of the model, relative to a simpler model and/or alternative approaches will need to be considered carefully. Third, the possibility that models with a large number of high-risk factors in them will prove unworkable must be considered before resources are committed.

THE TECHNICAL SYNOPSIS

Once it has been decided that a financial model is the correct approach, it is usually worth producing a brief technical synopsis of the proposed model. The purpose of this is, primarily, to provide a structure to work to in developing the model, but it will also serve as a further check on the technical risk involved, as well as allowing decisions on software and so on to be made.

There are five basic parts to the technical synopsis:

- data requirements and collection strategy (see Chapter 4)
- outline structure of model logic (see Chapter 5)
- outputs
- software (see Chapter 6)
- resource plan.

Data requirements

The maxim 'rubbish in: rubbish out' is too frequently forgotten in financial modelling. The quality and availability of data is of major importance to a successful model. Therefore, the plan must describe what data is required and where it is to come from. If tools such as workshops are to be used to gather data, then this should also be mentioned. The amount of data, and how it is structured, will also be key factors to note in the plan as this will determine how the model is to handle data analysis.

Outline of model logic

The model logic is the part of the model responsible for calculating results or, to put it another way, it is the means by which the model meets the business goals. So, the model plan must clearly state the functions that the model must provide in order to meet these requirements and how, in outline, it will do so. To do this, the plan may need to use a mix of description, diagrams and outline program flows in order to describe the logic path that will be taken.

Outputs

Models can become very large and cumbersome, particularly if there is a significant amount of data involved. In among this detail, it can be easy to lose sight of the key outputs that are required to meet the business goal. More often than not, these will include some form of financial statements and financial performance indicators, such as ROCE and NPV, but many other outputs, perhaps of a technical or business-specific nature, are also often used. These may include factors such as average plant utilization (which could have been affected by the demand profile input to, or calculated by, the model), sales analyses, price information, market share, staff numbers, ratio of direct to indirect staff and so on.

Software selection

The selection of modelling software is considered later in Part 3. However, it is important to recognize software as an issue at the planning stage. In most cases, a modeller will use the same software to build any model. This software is most likely to be a spreadsheet, such as Microsoft Excel, but it could be a more traditional financial modelling language, such as FCS, or one of a number of other options, such as Lotus Improv.

Different software approaches inevitably have their strengths and weaknesses. It may, therefore, be possible to match the strengths of a particular piece of software to the needs of a given model. Thus, the model plan should establish the criteria the modelling software requires and evaluate these against the capabilities of different software options. For example, if a model is expected to have frequent major changes to its logic, then the rigidity imposed by a modelling language might be inappropriate. However, if the requirement was for large amounts of data to be accessed from corporate databases, a modelling language might score highly. The merits of the various different types of software will be returned to in Chapter 6.

Resource plan

The final part of the model plan is to decompose the model development into a series of steps and to estimate the time scales for each step. The resource plan should also indicate dependencies external to the modelling process, such as 'budgets agreed'... and identify exactly who the users and modellers will be at each stage.

APPENDIX: EXAMPLE OF A PROPOSAL FOR A FINANCIAL MODEL

The situation

Browns Limited, a high street bank, is concerned that its structure of charges for current accounts results in a loss for certain groups of customer. Therefore, it is undertaking a study to consider alternative ways of charging.

Browns currently levies a £10 per month charge on all current accounts that become overdrawn during the previous month. No transaction fees are charged for any services, such as cheque encashment, cash withdrawal/deposit and standing orders. Each cheque processed costs the bank £0.34, each cash withdrawal/deposit costs £0.23 and administering a standing order costs £0.50 per month. Customers may overdraw by up to £500, for which interest is charged at 15 per cent. Accounts in credit receive interest at 5 per cent. The bank invests its cash balances at 10 per cent.

The bank's corporate planner has analysed the customer base and grouped them into three categories and each contains a third of the total current account customers. The results of the study are as follows.

Table 3.1

	Transaction		
Average balance	*Average number of cheques written*	*Average number of cash withdrawals or deposits*	*Average number of standing orders*
£630	7	6	3
£206	5	8	2
−£198	5	11	2

The planner calculates that the first group of customers each costs the bank £2.64, net, per month and the second group each costs the bank £4.02 per month. Only the third group returns any profit to the bank: £7.25 each per month. As there are 40 000 customers in each group, the bank therefore makes £22 400 per month profit on this service.

This figure represents a substantial cross-subsidization of the customers in credit by those with overdrafts. The bank would like to make a profit on *each* customer group, but realizes that changing the charging structure will also change its customers' behaviour and may result in some customers leaving the bank altogether.

Before deciding on a new charging structure, Browns decides to commission a study to determine how customers might react to changes in the changing structure. The most important variables are found to be (in order):

- other banks' policy on free banking
- charging structure of other banks
- length of time customers have banked with Browns
- the interest rates offered by Browns relative to other banks
- the number of Browns' cash machines relative to other banks.

The problem

Browns wishes to build a financial model to examine the profitability of different charging structures. The model is to look at the revenue effects of customers leaving the bank or changing their habits, as well as the changes in systems costs that will result from altering the charging structure.

The business case proposal

The business goal

What contribution to the bank will the proposed project make?
The objective of this study is to evaluate ways to improve the bank's profitability. This is to be achieved by targeting a reduction in the current losses made on the high- and average-balance customer account groups. The mechanism proposed to make this move is changes to the bank's charging structure.

The role of the proposed financial model

What role will a financial model play in achieving this goal?
A financial model is proposed to examine the impact of various possible changes in the charging structure on overall profitability. Relationships in

the model will replicate the impact of a number of key behaviours and events on profitability. This will enable a number of alternative charging structures to be examined.

The benefit of using a financial model is that the impact of a large variety of influences can be examined simultaneously, across a number of different options. The intention is that the model will also act as a focus for gathering information and provoking thought within the bank about the impact of different factors on average balances and transaction patterns.

The assessment of non-modelling options

Is a financial model the best means of achieving the goal above?

The two major issues that face any approach to this project are the availability and quality of base input data and the behavioural nature of the key decision variables. The proposed financial model is expected to be primarily a data manipulation tool and to provide focus for the project. Two basic questions must therefore be answered before deciding to proceed with building a model.

- Is a financial model the most effective focus for the exercise?
- Does a financial modelling approach provide greater added value, in relation to the resources required, than alternative analysis approaches?

Before addressing these questions, it is necessary to consider some of the possible alternative approaches to meeting the business goal. These fall into two basic camps. First, not attempting quantitative analysis, instead resorting to techniques such as ranking, perhaps making use of workshops and qualitative discussion papers. Second, using alternative qualitative techniques, for example multiple regression analysis to relate transaction volume to the key explanatory variables, such as the competing bank's charging policy.

Effective focus

A financial model compares favourably with the alternatives in terms of providing an effective focus. The main reason for this is the completeness financial modelling encourages. If the model is carefully specified, then deficiencies in data are made obvious and attention is immediately directed towards filling gaps. With a qualitative analysis, however, there is greater potential for incomplete analysis because linkages are less explicitly defined. The main advantage financial modelling has over other quantitative techniques, such as regression analysis, are that it can be understood easily and managers can relate to it without difficulty.

Added value

The added value of a financial model compared with qualitative techniques is that it produces a forecast in comparable, that is, financial, terms. A regression analysis shares this quality, but its output is more difficult to interpret and, hence, explain to managers in the bank.

Risk assessment

Are there any major risks in developing the proposed model? If so, identify them and assess their impact.
As already discussed, the main risk factors for the project lie with the financial model itself. If data quality can be guaranteed, then the actual mechanics of building the model itself are expected to be straightforward.

Recommendation

What are the next steps that should be taken?
Proceed to producing a technical synopsis for a financial modelling approach. This synopsis should consider data quality and availability issues in greater detail.

The technical synopsis

The data requirements and outline model structure

The historic data that will drive the model will come from Brown's Customer Transaction Database (CTD), held on the AS/400 computer system. This database stores the monthly average balance and the average number and amount of transactions by cash, cheque and standing order for each customer per month for the past 12 months.

Forecasts will be made by applying assumption information, such as 'Brown's abolishes free banking ahead of other banks', to a series of relationships that will translate those assumptions into changes to the historic behaviour as indicated by the CTD information. As a result, profitability will change.

The most demanding element of this model will be estimating the relationships. Estimating how each individual customer will react to a change is clearly neither possible nor practicable.Therefore, customers must be divided into manageable groups and each group assigned a particular behaviour. For example, customers who have been with the bank for a long time are less likely to move to another bank. It is believed that most of the customer information required is available in working papers that resulted from the recent customer survey. Further work will, however, be required to analyse that data.

Outputs

The output required from the model is:

- annual profit per customer group
- average balance per customer group
- volume and amount of each type of transaction per customer group.

Software

It is proposed that Brown's standard spreadsheet be used, linked to the CTD via the package's standard database driver. Macros will be used to enable the spreadsheet to query the database.

Resource plan

Client:	Charging Steering Group
Manager:	Planning Manager
Modeller:	Assistant Management Accountant
Start date:	02/03/9X
End date:	07/05/9X
Initial design by:	06/03/9X
Data ready by:	21/03/9X
Model built by:	30/04/9X
Tested by:	07/05/9X

4

COLLECTING AND WORKING WITH DATA

TYPES OF DATA

Introduction

Armed with a model plan, it is now time to consider the actual content of the model itself. All financial models can be thought of as comprising three basic sections:

- data section, which consists of a variety of types of input information
- logic section, that is, the relationships within the model that transform input data into the desired output, for example the statement 'variable costs = 40 per cent of sales' is a piece of logic
- output section, that is, the desired end result of the model, such as a cash flow or statement of key performance indicators.

Within each of these sections, there will be one or more subsections, or modules as they are called in Figure 4.1. For example, in the data section, there may be modules of operating cost, capital cost, sales, price and depreciation data, as well as one or more modules of assumptions covering

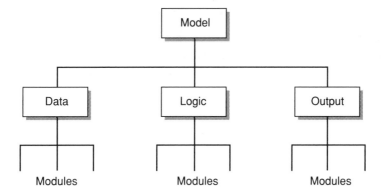

Figure 4.1 Outline of the model's structure

finance, tax, economic variables and so on. The logic section will contain modules to calculate revenue, forecast costs and so on. In the output section, there may be modules for the financial statements and for key performance indicators.

It is normal for most emphasis to be placed on producing working logic (see Chapter 5). From a model building point of view, this is entirely natural as the model is, to a large extent, defined by its logic. However, from a financial analysis standpoint, the logic on its own serves little purpose without sound input data. To use an analogy, if the logic is the engine of the model, the data is the fuel.

In many ways, the logic and data parts of the model are interconnected. To continue with the engine analogy, it is necessary to know what the characteristics of the fuel are before designing the engine and, before refining the fuel, it is important to know to what use it will be put. In practice, both these functions must, to a greater or lesser degree, be carried on in parallel. Nevertheless, it is important to establish a clear picture of what data is available to the model quite early on in the process so that the logic may be designed accordingly or further data-gathering exercises launched.

The fundamental purpose of a financial model is usually to gain a better understanding of what will happen in the future, that is to make a forecast. There are two broad approaches to forecasting with financial models. The first approach involves two stages:

- establish a base forecast, for example 'on the basis of current levels of competition and incorporating the product developments we already know about, demand is expected to grow at 5 per cent per annum over the next 3 years'
- examine various alternative scenarios, for example, 'if we were to reduce our price by 10 per cent, sales could be expected to rise by 8 per cent'.

The limitations of this, the sensitivity approach, were discussed in Chapter 1. The second approach is to use probabilities (see Chapter 2) and reduce the modelling to one stage. The types of data required by the two approaches will be similar and fall into three broad groups:

- *historic data* such as 'last year's staff cost was £205 330'
- *assumption data* such as 'the interest rate will be 10 per cent during the life of the project'
- *forecast data* such as 'next year's staff cost is expected to be £215 596'.

In addition to these basic types of data, that are common to both approaches, the sensitivity approach additionally requires *dynamic data*, such as 'each 1 per cent increase in price will result in a 0.8 per cent drop in sales'. The probability approach naturally enough needs *probability data*, such as 'sales are normally distributed around a mean of £4 million, with a standard deviation of £0.6 million'. Figure 4.2 illustrates the relationship between the types of data and forecasting for each approach. Each of these types of data are discussed further next.

Historic data

Although investment advisors may caution that the past is no guide to the future, most financial models rely heavily on historic data. Historic data is thought of as tangible, or real, and, therefore, gives a degree of comfort. Historic data is also the basis of most forecasting methods. For example, last period's sales figure might form the basis for an annual growth rate or, in a more sophisticated model, the last five years' monthly sales might be used to identify trends and seasonal patterns.

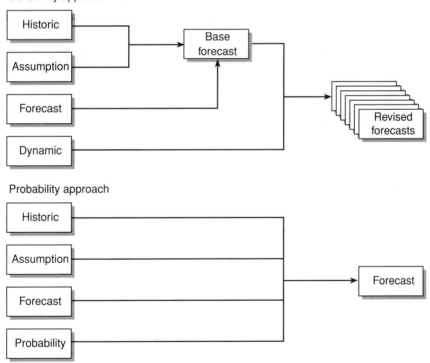

Figure 4.2 The types of data required for different approaches

Nevertheless, although historic data often gives the modeller a useful starting point, it may not always be available. For example, in the case of a new venture there will have been no sales made or costs incurred from which future trends could be estimated. In this case, much greater reliance will have to be placed on data from technical, market research and other forecast sources.

Assumption data

Most models will be based on a certain amount of historic information, such as past levels of costs, prices, demand and so on, to which a series of assumptions will be applied in order to make forecasts about the future. For example, examination of past sales figures might show that last year's sales were 1050 units and that, over the last 5 years, the growth in sales averaged 6 per cent per year. As a result, an assumption might be made that the historic trend will continue. The demand for next year is, therefore, forecast as $1050 \times 1.06 = 1113$ units.

Assumption data may be derived from three principle sources:

- based on historic information
- from management judgement (which may range from a 'finger in the air' guess, to a sound knowledge)
- from technical reports.

If historic data is used to formulate assumptions, then those assumptions may be modified subsequently in the light of management information.

Forecast data

If one method of building a financial model is to apply assumption data to historic data in order to make a forecast within the model, then an alternative method must be to input a forecast directly into the model itself. This will produce a much simplified model, but may also reduce the flexibility that the model has to examine different assumptions.

To illustrate this, consider choosing between using a trade association forecast of market size and using the model to calculate the market size, based on input data about changes in consumer preferences, new product launches and historic trends. The former is easy and the latter difficult to model, but if the variables that affect market size are part of the model, then the model is a more useful tool because it can look at the impact of changes to these variables of market size. The trade-off between modelling complexity and usefulness is often not an easy one to make. Over-ambition can be, and often is, fatal. Therefore before embarking on sophisticated modelling, it is important to ask a few basic questions.

- Do we need to be able to run changes through the model or can the variable be taken as given?
- What forecast data is available and how good is it?
- Do we know enough about the underlying processes to improve on it by modelling?
- Even if we know about the process, have we got enough basic data on the processes to complete the model?

In many ways, the first point is the key question, 'Should we do it?'. The others are 'Can we do it?' For example, if a model is intended to examine alternative financing structures, then a detailed representation of competitive aspects may be inappropriate. However, if the model is being used to decide whether or not to progress with a new strategy, then the impact of competition on NPV is likely to be more important than the impact of any special financing structures.

Nevertheless, even if the purpose of the model suggests that a variable is important, the nature of the relationships within it may mean that it is not. If this is the case, it would also be futile to put substantial effort into explaining that variable. The importance of individual variables can be established by means of simple sensitivity analysis. For example, if a firm's fixed costs are currently 75 per cent of its total costs and total costs amount to 80 per cent of sales, then the size of the fixed cost burden will clearly be an important variable to examine in the model.

Dynamic data

Once a base case model has been developed, then for the sensitivity approach, the next stage is to examine various potential scenarios. For example, 'Could we increase profits if we cut price by 5 per cent?' In order to answer these kinds of questions, information is needed that allows the model to react in some sensible fashion. Dynamic 'data' describes how variables should move in relation to each other. Therefore, if price is cut by x per cent, there might be direct impacts on the firm's sales as a result of customers switching from substitute products, but competitors might react to this and so on.

Probability data

In a probabilistic model, instead of running multiple scenarios, key variables are assigned a probability distribution using special software (such as a spreadsheet 'add on'). The software that does this runs the model many hundreds or thousands of times to produce expected values for key variables such as profit or NPV.

DATA REQUIREMENTS

Financial models are used for many different purposes. Indeed, applications of financial modelling are continually growing as it moves away from its traditional role in evaluating capital budgeting decisions in manufacturing industries and into fields such as strategy, planning and pricing – not just in manufacturing, but in the service sectors as well. This means that the sort of data required by models can vary widely. None the less, although the end objective of models may be different, most financial models have a fair degree of overlap in their content. Typically, models will require data in at least some of the following areas:

- technical
- market and competition
- costs – levels and structures
- financing, tax and working capital.

Technical data

Financial models aim to represent the real world in terms of flows of money. The real world they model is described in physical terms, such as the volume of output and number of staff employed. Therefore, financial models are often driven by technical, or engineering, data that must then be converted into financial terms. This is particularly the case with capital budgeting models, where the technical specification frequently defines the cost and revenue profiles of the project. For example, consider an engineering firm evaluating the replacement of old machines with a new, computer-controlled lathe. The new lathe will reduce set-up times, use materials more efficiently, be able to produce higher quality, more complicated cuts and will raise hourly output. Its ability to do this will be governed by its technical specification. Any financial model used to evaluate the new machine must, therefore, work from this specification, as this will be one of the main determinants of both revenue and cost.

This link between the technical specification and the business forecast (as represented by the financial model) is important in two ways. First, the technical specification may open up new business possibilities that the model must take into account. Perhaps in the case of the lathe, its greater cutting precision might allow work to be done in new product areas. Second, the technical specification will directly affect the cost and revenue calculations. If the new machine can produce more, then its revenue can, potentially, be greater. However, the machine might cost more to run in terms of power, maintenance or consumables. This relationship between output and cost will also need to be incorporated into the cost calculation.

Market and competition data

Business operates in a competitive environment: everything a firm does must, in some way, take account of the market-place. Financial models *should* reflect this. Too often, though, financial models pay scant attention to modelling the relevant competitive market. There are two common reasons for this. The first is uncertainty about future demand levels and competitors' actions, such as new product launches. Most firms have some idea about what is happening in the market, but few have the detailed quantitative data to translate this knowledge into a model. Second, there is often a fear that, even if data is available, competitive and market relationships are too complicated to model effectively. Although both these points are clearly valid, a financial model that does not take account of the competitive environment in some way must be viewed as grossly inadequate.

Because a firm's knowledge about competitors will always be limited, the sophistication of a model's treatment of market factors is constrained by the availability of data. Nevertheless, at least some data can normally be found. Sourcing this data is easier if data requirements are considered in two parts: general market data and company-specific competitor data.

General market data

This data is concerned with the overall parameters of a market. These include features such as total market size, number and size of competitors (that is, market shares), barriers to new firms entering the market and homogeneity of products. This type of data is reasonably widely available and can be used, for example, to link the firm's demand to the overall size of the market, instead of simply assuming that firms operate in some vacuum. The application of such data is discussed further in Chapter 5.

Although using general market data to improve the realism of a model is often desirable, it may not always be appropriate. For example, consider an insurance company that markets a range of vehicle insurance policies. The size of its market will be determined by factors such as people's concerns about burglary, the cost of cover, legislation and the degree to which they can provide more effective (or cheaper) protection via car alarms, removable radios and so on. Typically, one firm will have little influence over the total market size. It could be argued, therefore, that in this case, there is little point modelling determinants of market size.

However, even when one type of market data is not relevant, it may still be important to include others. In the insurance example, market share may be more within the control of the firm and so may be usefully modelled. Insurance is primarily a 'commodity' product, that is one insurance is much the same as another. Market share will, therefore, be affected primarily by price relative to that of competitors. Other factors, such as reputation for fair dealing, prompt payment, shops on the high street, easy terms and image built by advertising may also be important. In all cases, though, it will be the insurer's position *relative* to the competitors that determines it's share of the market.

In summary, then, giving thought to the application of general market data can improve the realism, and therefore usefulness, of a model quite simply.

Company-specific competitor data

Knowledge about specific competitors can raise the usefulness of models further. On one level, competitor information is quite easy to gather – for example, competitors' prices. However, on its own, such data is not all that much use to a model because it does not convey any notion of the relationship between, say, competitor price and the firm's demand. The *really* valuable competitor data concerns competitor reactions. However, such information is typically difficult to obtain, may be unreliable and is difficult to build into a financial model.

To illustrate this point, consider the insurance example once more. As far as modelling is concerned, the key questions for the insurer will be 'How much will my market share move if I reduce premiums by x per cent relative to my competitors?' and 'What response can I expect from them and how will it affect my share?' Similar questions might also be asked about the impact of advertising, opening new shops and so on. The key concept here is that, to use a model dynamically, it will be necessary to model the *respon-*

siveness of market share to price and other changes. In this example, a survey of British motorists[1] showed that 27 per cent of them would be willing to switch insurer for a 5 per cent cut in premium. The insurer's model would, therefore, be wise to include this fact as a variable, although, in addition, the model would need to describe what competitors would do in response to such a move.

Cost data

The cost section of many financial models is where most detail is to be found. It is quite common to come across models that look rather like this.

Table 4.1

	1993	1994	1995	1996
Revenue	100	125	140	155
Costs				
Electricity	3.01	3.47	3.99	4.21
Stationery	1.22	1.88	2.12	2.32
Computer supplies	5.79	6.09	6.67	6.93
Rent	10.67	12.11	12.91	14.10
Rates	4.00	4.72	5.31	5.66
Basic pay	53.69	59.38	66.82	72.59
Overtime	12.34	17.65	23.00	27.01
Pension	10.19	12.88	13.77	14.55

In this model, revenue looks as though it has been roughly guessed at, while costs are calculated at a comparatively low level of detail. This is natural enough – costs are largely internal to the firm and therefore something about which more is known than demand. There is nothing wrong with specifying costs in detail, however, as accurate cost estimates can only improve the validity of the model. None the less, a better balance of effort often needs to be struck between getting the 'easy' part – the costs – right and addressing the more tricky questions of demand.

Although it may not be necessary to build in logic that allows a model to examine the exact details of changes in the structure of business rates, it will still be important that costs properly reflect the technical aspects of the project, (as discussed above), and the level of output. Modelling different technical options, where this is applicable, will probably involve substituting a completely new set of cost assumptions into the model for each major technical option. However, the response of variable costs to changes in demand will need to be much more flexible. Therefore, a basic distinction between fixed, variable and semi-variable costs (the 'cost structure') must be established in the model.

Deciding what costs are fixed, and therefore will not change with the level of output, and which are variable with output, is a subject that occupies many pages of basic economics textbooks. The two key aspects of cost structure for financial modelling purposes are:

- the nature of the output – cost relationship, such as linear, curve, stepped, kinked
- limits within which each cost is really fixed.

Taking the cost relationship issue first. Variable costs are typically assumed to include costs such as timber for a furniture manufacturer, computer consumables for a consultancy and casual labour for a building contractor. They are costs that show a direct relationship to output, whether that output is tables and chairs, management reports or new roads. They have as defining characteristics the facts that they would not occur if there was no output and that they rise as output does. However, for a variety of reasons, they may not rise *directly* as output does. To illustrate this, consider the following examples.

- Elements of cost may have to be incurred in fixed lumps. For example, buying bricks is a variable cost of house building, but it may be that bricks can only be ordered in quantities of, say 10 000. Therefore, if only 150 bricks are needed, 10 000 must still be ordered. In this case, the cost relationship is 'stepped'.
- Some costs may rise more slowly than output. Examples of costs that decrease as output rises are quite commonplace as a result of the discounts given for quantity.
- Costs can also rise more rapidly than output and, although this is less common than the case above, examples do exist. The classic case is when a good is in short supply and, as demand increases, costs rise, too. An example might be a software firm providing leading edge software advice that requires the use of computer programmers with highly specialized skills. As the amount of consultancy work rises and, hence, more of these

specialists are employed, so the salaries they can demand also rises. A more common example is labour cost, which may rise by more than output due to the effects of overtime payments, which are above the basic rate.

The second point concerns the limits of the fixed cost assumptions. Basic economics textbooks are fond of saying that, in the long run, no costs are fixed – factories can be sold or built, staff laid off and even technology can change. Even without going to quite that limit, it is fairly obvious that a production line, for example, has a certain amount of flexibility in its output – perhaps an extra shift can be introduced, or some non-essential maintenance delayed. However, if demand rises above a certain level, an additional line will be required. Therefore, although for most practical purposes the capital cost of the line (as represented by depreciation) can be considered fixed, there will be limits.

Financing, tax and working capital data

The final data section of the financial model is concerned with purely financial aspects. How is money going to be raised? How much tax will be paid and what levels will working capital run at? By definition, this section is perhaps rather more concerned with logic than data. The data that is required will cover such topics as interest and fee rates, loan repayment schedules, target gearing ratios, tax rates and regulations and debtor/creditor/stock days. Mostly these variables will simply be input assumptions.

SOURCES OF INFORMATION

Introduction

So far, the sort of data that will be required by a financial model has been discussed. It was said that data breaks into three basic types: assumptions, historic and forecast, plus the two approach-specific types of dynamic and probability. Sources of assumptions data have been briefly discussed. Forecast data will be derived based on historic data that has been adjusted to take account of ways in which we believe historic patterns may change. Forecasting and other data analysis will be examined in the next section, so in this section the focus will be on the remaining category and examine sources of historic data. Sources of technical data will not be considered as it is assumed that this information will come from consulting engineers, manufacturers' data sheets and so on. In other words, it will effectively be a 'black box' that the modeller will often be required simply to accept.

Sources of market and competitive data

Models tend not to explicitly model market and competitive considerations because data is difficult to obtain. However, the difficulty really lies in the complexities of the logic. Basic historic data, such as current market size, is easier to come by. Sources include:

- government publications
- direct queries to government departments
- own staff – particularly sales and customer service staff
- specifically commissioned market research or consultancy – using either internal or external resources
- commercial data providers
- industry and trade associations
- 'think tank' and research institute reports
- academic research – published and otherwise.

Government sources

Most governments publish a vast array of economic and business statistics that can be of use to financial models. The European Commission also publish large volumes of statistics concerning the Community. Government statistics vary widely in their usefulness. For example, some are essentially macro-economic and so of little use for the average financial model. However, there is also a wealth of useful information on prices, costs, trade, specific industries, population, spending and so on, that can be very useful, particularly in demand estimation.

As well as these business statistics, governments may also commission special studies that while not always being intended for business purposes, may be very useful and will be far less costly than the equivalent commercially produced information. An example of this is a study by the Office of Population Censuses and Surveys (OPCS) into alcohol consumption.[2] Although this study was primarily designed to examine the social and health problems caused by drinking, it also provides a breakdown of alcohol consumption by age, sex, social class and so on – all perfect information to use as a starting point for macro forecasting of the drinks market (an example that is developed in the Appendix to this chapter).

Although government data is cheap and usually highly authoritative, it is not without problems. Government macro-economic forecasts are often criticized as being inaccurate. Statistics, such as RPI and unemployment figures, have been the subject of various, apparently politically motivated, changes in recent years. Government data is also criticized for not being produced in a timely fashion. For example, the Central Statistical Office's Family Expenditure Survey is potentially a tremendously important data source for market planning, but it is frequently several years out of date. Nevertheless, despite these problems, government publications provide access to a wealth of statistical material, much of it at quite low levels of detail and some of it not available elsewhere. A full list of UK government and EC publications is available from HMSO.

If government publications fail to provide the information required in the correct format, or if figures for extra years are required, it is often fruitful to approach the department in question directly. Many departments will be very helpful in meeting requests for information, although a fee may be charged for any work involved.

Using the firm's staff

Frequently, one of the best sources of information about what is happening in the market and competitors will come from the firm's own staff, particularly from those who 'face the market' by interacting with customers in sales or service roles. However, making the link between the staff responsible for a financial model and the operational staff with customer and competitor knowledge is often not something that companies are geared up for. Improving these links is worth while though. Various methods are available, such as questionnaires, suggestion schemes, workshops or even just informal chats. To encourage communication, some form of reward scheme may even be appropriate for the best information or ideas.

Although using the firm's own staff has many benefits – such as providing inside knowledge of the market, being cheap and perhaps motivating those asked to participate – the results of such exercises must still be treated with care. One reason for this is the danger of 'group think'. This is a tendency that has been identified by psychologists studying group behaviour and means that minority views are actively suppressed so as to conform to a dominant group view. Thus, for example, a close-knit sales team might well develop group think about what they believe competitors are likely to do. A model that perpetuates what may be misguided thinking serves no one.

Market research and other commercial data sources

Market research can be carried out as an in-house study, can be bought in from third parties as a specially commissioned project or can be purchased as limited-circulation sector reports. Specially commissioned research is expensive, but it is nevertheless a very closely targeted use of resources and so can be highly cost-effective.

Several market research firms specialize in providing ready-made market reports that are often a good source of information about market size, among other data. Although these reports can be very useful for markets with which the firm is unfamiliar, they typically cost several hundred pounds and the analysis can be rather superficial to those with more than a basic understanding of the market. One of the largest suppliers of these reports is Key Note. Other sources include subsidiaries of the Financial Times and the Economist publications. As well as industry data the Economist publishes very useful country information in book form. Industry and trade associations also gather statistics on individual markets that have been gathered from their members in the industry.

As well as specially commissioned research and published reports, various computerized data sources provide important, particularly financial, information. These services are of two broad types:

- on-line, where the user is connected via a telephone line and modem to a database held by an information provider
- on CD-ROM, which, essentially, is a means of storing a very large database on a compact disk that may then be accessed by individual PCs. Datastream is an example of an on-line service, while the ICC database is provided on CD-ROM. Both provide company and other financial information and both are quite expensive. While on-line services normally charge for each enquiry, CD-ROM has the advantage that, once the subscription has been paid, unlimited use may be made of the disk.

Academic sources

Academic sources span both the university/college sector and privately funded research institutes and think tanks. There is a surprisingly wide range of useful data that is available from the academic sector. This falls into the following main categories:

- empirical studies, which may cover a huge range of topics, and although many of these are rather esoteric for business purposes, much industry-specific research does also take place and this may provide very useful analyses such as estimates of demand elasticity and forecast demand functions

- data collation and analysis services, such as the London Business School Risk Management Service which provides estimates of beta for the CAPM, and the Henley Centre for Forecasting
- reports, analysing market or industry prospects and trends.

The major problem with academic sources is that it is often difficult to find out exactly what is available where. Therefore, if academic information is likely to be a useful source, it is important to establish contacts with key management schools.

Sources of cost data

Cost data typically comes from the accounting system, although, for new projects, technical reports and management estimates may also play a significant part. Although this seems rather straightforward compared with the processes that are required to gain market information, the basic data that is available from these systems may not always be of use without further work. In some cases, such as government departments and agencies that do yet operate commercial accounting systems, cost data may have to be estimated by means of special studies.

Because data from the accounting system, and in particular the management accounting system, is so important for financial modelling, it is important that modellers are aware of its potential problems.

DATA ANALYSIS

Introduction

The data sources referred to above will yield both historic and forecast data. However, there will be occasions when further manipulation of the base data will be needed – perhaps for forecasting sales, estimating costs or assessing likely competitive reactions. Some of the methods that can be used to forecast sales and costs are shown in Figure 4.3.

The matrix in Figure 4.3 classifies data analysis methods by the type of data they use and the approach they take. It is beyond the scope of this book to examine all these approaches and so discussion here will be primarily limited to a brief overview of some analytical methods. Two types of analytical technique are identified in the matrix. The first, multivariate methods, is the term for a family of techniques that simultaneously analyse several dif-

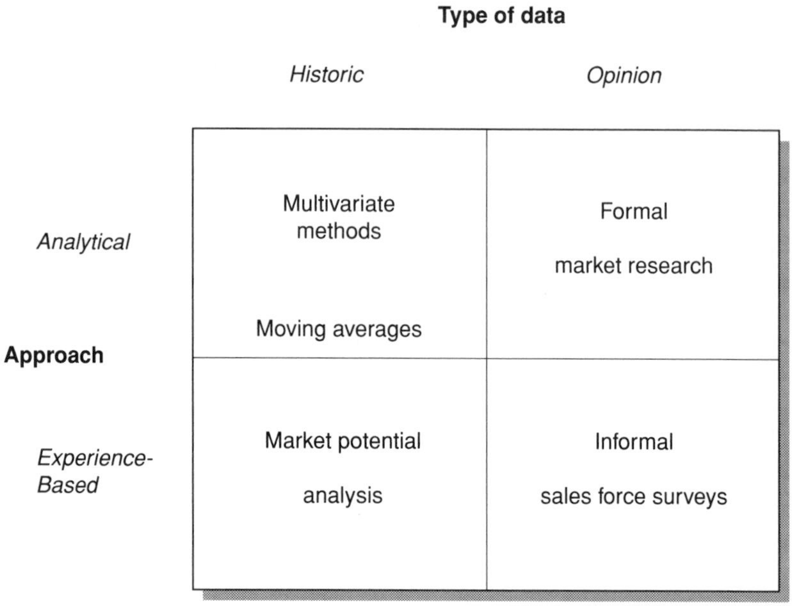

Type of data

	Historic	*Opinion*
Analytical	Multivariate methods Moving averages	Formal market research
Experience-Based	Market potential analysis	Informal sales force surveys

Approach

Figure 4.3 Methods of data analysis

ferent variables. The most commonly known technique is multiple regression analysis (MRA), the application of which will be looked at briefly below. Other multivariate methods include discriminant analysis, factor analysis and cluster analysis.[3] The second technique listed is the use of moving averages. Moving averages provide a simple way of forecasting and are ideally suited to use in financial models, especially those models based on spreadsheets.

Moving averages

Simple moving averages

The assumption underlying forecasts based on moving averages is that sales for future periods can be estimated as an average of past periods. For example, Table 4.2 shows a three-monthly moving average[4] of monthly sales figures.

Table 4.2

Month	Sales	Three-monthly moving average
January	100	–
February	170	(100 + 170 + 180)/3 = 150
March	180	(170 + 180 + 205)/3 = 185
April	205	(180 + 205 + 245)/3 = 210
May	245	(205 + 245 + 270)/3 = 240
June	270	(245 + 270 + 265)/3 = 260
July	265	(270 + 265 + 170)/3 = 235
August	170	(265 + 170 + 240)/3 = 225
September	240	(170 + 240 + 265)/3 = 225
October	265	(240 + 265 + 290)/3 = 265
November	290	(265 + 290 + 180)/3 = 245
December	180	–

The moving average used in this example gives equal weight to each period. However, for forecasting purposes, more emphasis is often given to later periods. The reason for this is that they are less distant and so it is assumed that they most accurately reflect what will happen in the future. Of course, while this might well be true, it might also reflect seasonal variation in sales. In this example, for instance, sales drop off around Christmas and in the August holiday season. It would, therefore, be inappropriate to take the December figure as indicating a shift in the trend. In this kind of series, it is first necessary to identify the seasonal component and isolate it (a method of doing this is discussed below).

If it is decided to give greater emphasis to later periods, there are two main ways of doing this. The most straightforward way is simply to calculate a weighted moving average. This is done by multiplying each period's figure by a weight (where the sum of the weights is 1) before calculating the moving average. The choice of weights in this method is arbitrary. An alternative method, which avoids the problem of arbitrary weights, is called *exponential smoothing*.

Exponentially smoothed moving averages

Exponential smoothing is a broadly similar idea to that of a simple weighted average, but, instead of having to decide on a different weight for each period, only one weight is required. The technique then automatically weights more recent values more. The method works by first selecting a weight between 0 and 1. The greater the weight chosen, the fewer periods are taken into account and, consequently, the less smoothed the series will be. The formula for calculating each average is as follows:

$$\bar{y}_t = \alpha y_t + (1 - \alpha)\bar{y}_{t-1}$$

where:
$\bar{y}_t$ = weighted average for period t
y_t = actual sales for period t
$\bar{y}_{t-1}$ = weighted average for period $t - 1$
α = weight

Using a weight (α) of around 0.2 - 0.4 seems to produce the best compromise between smoothing and placing more emphasis on recent data. To give little weight to past data *and* to produce a smoothed trend, then it is possible to calculate one set of exponentially weighted averages, based on a low weight of say 0.1, and then to produce another set, with a higher α, using the previously calculated data. This is called *double exponential smoothing*.

Removing seasonality from a time series

It was noted earlier that there might be a seasonal component to sales that would have to be removed before a usable trend could be derived. There are, in fact, four components that make up a time series, such as sales. As well as trend and seasonality, there are possible random effects and the impact of the business cycle. The method for isolating the seasonal and other components is worked through below using monthly data (the approach would be similar for quarterly data).

- *Step 1* Calculate a 12-monthly average for each year. Because this is over a yearly period it excludes seasonal variations.
- *Step 2* Divide each original monthly value by the trend value for that year. This leaves out the seasonal and random components.
- *Step 3* Compute the average of the values arrived at in Step 2. For example, if monthly data is used and there is three years' information, then calculate an average for January, an average for February and so on. The purpose of this is to remove the random component.
- *Step 4* Factor up each of the monthly results computed in Step 3 so that they total 12 (this is for monthly data, it would be 4 for quarterly data and so on). Thus, if the total of the indices calculated in Step 3 is 11.9, then multiply each index by 12 ÷ 11.9.
- *Step 5* Divide each of the original data by the index from Step 4. This removes the seasonal element from the series.

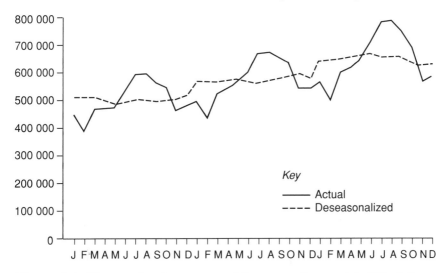

Figure 4.4 Thousands of passenger kilometres flown with UK airlines 1988–90 data with and without the seasonal element.

As an example, Figure 4.4 shows the demand for UK airlines[5], and clearly shows seasonal and trend components, both with and without the seasonal component removed.

Regression analysis

Another common method of examining trends in sales data is regression analysis. Regression analysis is a technique in which the effect of one or more independent variables on a single dependent variable is examined. If there is more than one independent variable, it is known as multiple regression analysis (MRA). MRA can be used, for example, to 'explain' the relationship between sales and influences such as price, average family income, competitors' prices, and so on. It is worth knowing at least something about the use of regression because it is such a widespread technique.

In its simplest form regression provides an alternative to the moving average methods discussed above. Most spreadsheets provide a function that uses regression to calculate a line of 'best fit'. The best fit line for the airline example is shown in Figure 4.5.

This line of best fit will, most commonly, be estimated by what is called the 'method of least squares'. All this means is that the calculation works out the position of the straight line that minimizes the total size of the (squared) differences between the line and the actual points.[6] The mechanics

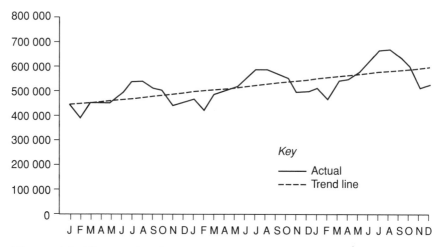

Figure 4.5 Thousands of passenger kilometres flown with UK airlines 1988–90 data with line of best fit found by means of regression analysis.

of the method are not important here as they are usually taken care of by the software. The interpretation of the result *is* significant, though, and before attempting any large-scale regression analysis, it is important to have a sound understanding of the assumptions underlying the method and the potential problems that may arise. Econometrics, as this discipline is called, is a fairly complicated subject, but there are a number of useful books available[7] that will provide guidance.

The airline example above is a case of the simplest type of regression – one variable is linearly related to just one other. In this case, because passenger kilometres flown was related to time, the regression is known as a *time series* model. A second type of regression analysis is known as the *cross-sectional* model. In this model one variable, passenger kilometres in this case, is related to a number of other 'explanatory' variables. It might be postulated for example that changes in the number of passenger kilometres flown are related to average disposable income and the real cost of air transport. A cross-sectional regression could be run to test this theory.

A variety of means are available for testing the statistical validity of regression models. Once these have been applied and a suitably validated model derived, be that time series or cross-sectional, the model can be used for forecasting purposes. In the case of the time series model, this will, essentially, consist of extending, or 'extrapolating', the line forward into the future. The cross-sectional model produces a forecast based on input assumptions about how the explanatory variables move.

Less analytical methods

In reality, most managers think that moving averages are a waste of time, far less multiple regression or the other, even less well-known, multivariate techniques. One of the main reasons for this is the complexity, both real and imagined, of the techniques and the fairly huge amounts of data that are required. A time series, for example, normally requires five years of monthly data. A more commonly used technique, therefore, is to examine the total potential of the market and then forecast the firm's share of that market. This two-stage approach is illustrated in the Appendix to this chapter by means of an example concerning the potential demand for wine in the UK. The example also shows some of the data sources that can be used.

APPENDIX: AN EXAMPLE OF MARKET ANALYSIS

This example shows how a fairly rough and ready forecast of market size might be made. The market chosen for this example is the UK market for wine sold in off licences (as opposed to in pubs and restaurants). The example was produced using readily available information, mostly that from either government sources or available in business libraries. The following sources were used.

Table 4.3

Reference	Source
1	CSO, 'Family Spending: A Report on the 1990 Family Expenditure Survey', HMSO, 1991.
2	CSO, 'Social Trends', 22, HMSO, 1992.
3	NTC, 'The Drink Pocket Book 1991'.
4	Key Note, 'Wine', ninth edition,1991/
5	OPCS, 'Drinking in England and Wales in the Late 1980s', Eileen Goddard, HMSO, 1991.
6	OPCS, '1989 – based Sub-national Population Projections (England)', HMSO, 1991.

The reports by NTC and Key Note are commercial sources and cost between £30 and well over £100 each. The others are all government sources and cost from around £5 to £25 each. The use of the commercial sources was confined to confirming market sizes. This information might also be available at less cost from trade associations. At the other end of the spectrum, market research reports on the industry may cost several thousand pounds each.

Examination of the available data helped decide what approach to adopt. A three-stage process was selected. The references that provided the base data are given in parentheses.

Step 1: Estimate current wine consumption

- Begin with *per capita* alcohol consumption (in units of alcohol), analysed by age and sex (3).
- Determine the proportion of this consumption that is wine (3).
- Calculate the total amount of alcohol, and hence wine, consumed (6).
- Translate this figure into bottles of wine, based on the average alcohol content of a bottle (3).
- Apply an average bottle price to determine the current market size in £ (3).
- Compare derived figure with other estimates to check validity and refine forecast if necessary (1,2,3 and 4).

Step 2: Forecast future consumption based on demographic changes

- Determine population forecasts by age and sex (6).
- Apply the changes to the consumption figures estimated above.

Step 3: Adjust forecasts based on qualitative assessments

- Adjust for changes in total alcohol consumption, due to factors such as health consciousness, improved acceptability of non-alcoholic drinks.
- Adjust for changes in wine's share of total consumption.
- Adjust for changes due to changes in income and socio-economic class.

Step 1: estimate current wine consumption

The starting point for the analysis was provided by the OPCS report on drinking. It was the result of a government study that, essentially, was concerned with alcohol and health. However, it also provides the information on both total alcohol and wine consumption we seek. It is also analysed by age and sex, which will be important for examining the potential effect of demographic changes on demand. For flexibility in modelling, it is decided to express *per capita* wine consumption as a percentage of total alcohol consumption, as follows.

Table 4.4

Age Alcohol Consumption	16–17	18–24	25–34	35–44	45–54	55–64	65–74	75+
Total (men)	7.2	20.1	18.5	17.8	13.3	11.6	8.3	5.8
Total (women)	4.53	7.26	5.59	5.64	3.69	3.02	2.94	1.87
%wine (men)	3%	4%	8%	11%	10%	12%	8%	6%
%wine (women)	14%	22%	38%	37%	31%	29%	18%	12%

This tells us the average number of units of alcohol consumed per person in each of the age bands per week(1 unit of alcohol is taken to be 10ml).

The next step is to translate these *per capita* figures into total figures. This was done by applying the populations in each age band (from OPCS population projections) to the figures, so giving total consumption figures. The population figures (in 000s) given are as follows.

Table 4.5

Age	16–24	25–34	35–44	45–54	55–64	65–74	75+
Males	4009.8	4215.3	3845.1	3114.8	2793.1	2186.3	1309.4
Females	3851.7	4144.0	3835.0	3117.1	2942.4	2721.9	2542.0

Unfortunately the age ranges do not quite tie up in the under 25 category and, therefore, it was decided to make an adjustment to the alcohol consumption figures. An average of the 16-17 and 18-24 consumption figures was taken, weighted by the number of years in each category. The result was as follows.

Table 4.6

Age	Male	Female
16 – 24	$(2 \times 7.2 + 7 \times 20.1) \div 9$ $= 17.2$	$(2 \times 4.53 + 7 \times 7.26) \div 9$ $= 6.65$

The total consumption of wine can now be calculated to be 3605 million units of alcohol per annum. An average alcohol content of 10.4 per cent is estimated and a bottle size of 750 ml assumed. This gives a demand of 466.9

million bottles or £1 283.98 million, at an average price of £2.20 per bottle. These figures were compared to estimates in the market research publications and found to be in broad agreement with them, which gives confidence in methodology adopted.

Step 2: make initial forecast

Having established the model for how demand is to be built up and verified it by calculating *current* demand, adjustments can be made to the input data to forecast *future* demand. These adjustments are of two sorts. First, demographic changes using government forecasts – these are made in this step. Then, in step 3, changes based on intuition, experience and or knowledge of the market are made.

As most people know, the demographic make up of the population is changing. In the case of a product such as wine, this is of critical importance as consumption patterns vary widely between age groups. It is, therefore, of interest to examine this effect on its own. The OPCS population projections provide the necessary input. Recalculating demand based on these changes produces the following forecast.

Table 4.7

Year	Million bottles
1989	462.3
1996	472.9
2001	478.9

Step 3: make qualitative adjustments to forecast

We now have a base forecast. However, many other factors will be at work in determining the demand for wine. At this stage, some of these can be brought into the forecast. This process inevitably involves a fair degree of guesstimation. Nevertheless, it is important to avoid invalidating the forecast at this stage through wild guesswork.

In the case of wine, there are a number of factors that may be expected to have an impact on demand. These are primarily social and cultural, which make them difficult to assess. For example, growing health consciousness might be expected to reduce alcohol consumption, but it is very difficult to be clear about the strength of the relationship and about whether wine might fare better or worse than the average for alcoholic drinks. Another potential factor is that male wine consumption is low in the UK in relation to many other European countries. This suggests that there is scope for increase.

There are many ways in which the effects of these factors could be estimated. For example market research could be used to assess attitudes or some form of multivariate technique could be applied to examine the correlation between growing concerns about the effect of alcohol on health and demand. These would be expensive and time-consuming solutions and, though, they might be appropriate in some cases, in many they would be rather akin to using a sledgehammer to crack a nut.

An alternative solution is to work with the data we have already got and try to estimate the impact of each change separately. For example, if it is believed that increased European integration will have an effect on male wine consumption, then the potential of this could be found by substituting in EC *per capita* consumption. It would then be a matter of judgement to in making an assessment of how quickly and to what extent this potential could be realized.

Notes

[1] Louis Harris International, *A Survey of Motor Insurance*, Sentry Insurance Co.,1977.

[2] OPCS, *Drinking in England and Wales in the Late 1980s,* HMSO, 1991.

[3] These are complicated techniques and, although sophisiticated computer software can make them more accessible, their use requires a good knowledge of the theory underlying their construction and use. A very good application-oriented guide to their use can be found in Hair, J.F., Anderson, R.E., Tatham, R.L., and Black, W.C., *Multivariate Data Analysis With Readings*, third edition, Macmillan, 1992.

[4] Any period can be chosen for a moving average, but the longer the period, the more smoothing the effect.

[5] Data from CSO, *Monthly Digest of Statistics,* 552.

[6] The explanation of the squared component is simply that it makes the deviations above and below the line positive.

[7] Some useful books include Gujarati, D.N., *Basic Econometrics*, second edition; Pindyck, R.S., and Rubinfeld, D.L., *Econometric Models and Economic Forecasts*, third edition; Davis, E.J., *Practical Sales Forecasting*; Granger, C.W.J., *Forecasting in Business and Economics,* second edition. Unfortunately, with the exception of Davis's book, these are all fairly difficult, reflecting the complexity of the subject.

5

DESIGN OF MODEL LOGIC

INTRODUCTION

Chapter 4 introduced the concept of financial models consisting of three sections. This chapter will focus on the most complicated of these – the logic. The logic section is where the bulk of the model's work will take place. For example, historic data will be turned into forecasts, the business impact of technical configurations will be calculated and financing and tax implications analysed.

The logic modules can vary from one model to the next, but a typical set of modules for a model includes:

- revenue
- operating costs
- working capital
- capital costs
- assets and depreciation
- tax
- financing.

THE REVENUE MODULE

The revenue module serves two main purposes. The first is to rearrange input data into the required output format. In its simplest terms, this might involve multiplying selling price by quantity sold to give revenue. Its second role is to project forward, based on input data. For example, if this year's sales, next year's forecast growth in those sales and the expected selling price are input into the data section, then the revenue module would use this information to calculate next year's revenue.

Although the basic derivation of revenue – price multiplied by quantity sold – is quite simple, there are several possible complexities to the basic equation. These take two main forms:

- *multidimensional analysis* for example, sales forecasts may be based on data input by product, which must then be translated into output by region as part of the output
- *forecasting method* the method of deriving the quantity sold that is used by the revenue calculation may range from simple guesswork to complicated econometric estimation to modelling the interaction of all firms within the market.

It is beyond the scope of this book to examine sophisticated forecasting methods (some simpler techniques have already been discussed in Chapter 4), so the discussion here will concentrate on exploring what is probably the most common approach to revenue – the use of growth rates to derive estimates of future sales or revenues.

Methods of forecasting using growth rates

There are several possible methods for using growth rates to forecast future revenues. In its simplest form, the most recent 'actual' sales statistics are multiplied by an assumed annual percentage increase to forecast the next period's sales. This process is then repeated for subsequent years, giving compound growth. The growth rate used can be either applied to unit sales (such as 1000 washing machines were sold last year, next year's sales are forecast to be 1000 + 10 per cent or, 1100 units), and then revenue calculated as price multiplied by unit sales, or the growth rate can be applied direct to the revenue figure (for example, revenue from the washing machines was £200 000, therefore forecast revenue is £220 000). In the latter case any changes in price cannot be examined and so the method is rather crude, but it is common none the less.

A slightly more sophisticated method is to derive sales as market size multiplied by market share and then to apply a separate growth rate to each in order to predict subsequent periods. This method gives more control as different influences can be applied to market size and the firm's share of that market. Nevertheless, unless reliable data is available, there can be no increase in the predictive power of the model from the added complexity of two growth rates.

Deciding which growth rates to use

Growth rates are often used because, as well as being easy to apply, they require very little information to drive them. However, financial models are often built with the intention of examining revenue from a number of view-points, perhaps being split by product, customer or by geographic sales area. If this is the case, then the growth rates used must also be available to that level of analysis. This may seem a simple point, but it is a common mistake in financial models to implicitly assume that revenue analysed by product, area, customer and so on will all increase at the same growth rate, despite the fact that the growth rate used probably only applies to one of them. Unless this difficulty is addressed explicitly in the model, then highly mis-leading results can be produced. To illustrate this, consider the following example, which shows data split by market, customer type and product.

Example An advanced computer software firm sells two products, an 'object-ori-ented' programming language and a neural network simulation. Last year the income from these was £5.7 million and £8.1 million respectively. The products were sold into several countries, producing the following sales figures:

	Language	Simulation
UK	£2.95m	£2.66m
France	£1.03m	Nil
USA	Nil	£3.90m
Japan	Nil	£1.54m
Australia	£1.72m	Nil

Sales are to two different types of customer: private individuals (such as researchers) and companies. An analysis of the <u>revenue</u> shows that the split between these two groups varies by country. UK revenue is 20 per cent to private customers and 80 per cent to corporate clients. Japanese and Australian sales are solely to corporate clients. French revenue is split 50:50 between private and corporate clients and USA revenue is 80 per cent from individuals and 20 per cent from corporate customers. The language retails for £199 and the simulation for £499 to corporate clients and for 75 per cent of these prices to private clients. (Local taxes, such as VAT, and exchange rate differentials are ignored for the purposes of this example.)

Industry predictions forecast a world-wide increase of 30 and 120 per cent in the use of object-oriented languages and neural network simulations respectively. However, marketing records suggest that sales in Japan and France typically grow 50 per cent slower than in the other markets (that is by 15 and 60 per cent respec-tively).

It is anticipated that prices in Europe and America will be able to be maintained next year with no loss of market share, but that in Japan and Australia prices for the language will have to fall by 25 per cent and for the simulation by 10 per cent in order to preserve market share.

In this case, the revenue and prices are known, but the volumes sold are not. In order to model future years, first it will be necessary to derive the volumes sold analysed by product and customer group across each market, as below.

Table 5.1

Unit sales		Product analysis		Customer analysis	
Country	Type	Language	Simulation	Private	Corporate
UK	Private	3953	1422	5375	–
	Corporate	11859	4265	–	16124
France	Private	3451	–	3451	–
	Corporate	2588	–	–	2588
USA	Private	–	8337	8337	–
	Corporate	–	1563	–	1563
Japan	Private	–	–	–	–
	Corporate	–	3086	–	3086
Australia	Private	–	–	–	–
	Corporate	8643	–	–	8643
Total		30494	18672	17162	32004

Revenue is defined as unit sales multiplied by price, therefore unit sales will equal revenue divided by price. All the information that is needed to calculate this at product, country and customer level is provided in the example. For instance, the figure of 3953 units of the language sold to private customers in the UK was calculated as follows:

$$\text{Unit sales} = (\text{UK revenue} \times \% \text{ private})/(\text{UK private customer price})$$
$$= (\pounds2,950,000 \times 0.2)/\pounds149.25$$
$$= 3,953.10 \text{ units}$$

When it comes to projecting next year's revenue, growth rates are available that will enable revenue to be analysed by product. However, to then assume that sales in each country and to each customer group will move *pro rata* is not justified by the data provided in the example. That is not to say that in the absence of better information, it cannot be done, merely that, if it were, then caution would need to be taken when analysing the results and making decisions based on it.

From a modelling viewpoint, if data on growth rates is available by product, customer and country, then the situation can become more complicated, because it is difficult to know which rate should be used to 'drive' the model. For example, assume that, in addition to the information on product growth rates and the limited piece of information about Japan and France having slower take up rates, it is believed that sales to private individuals will drop next year by 10 per cent in the UK and France and by 5 per cent in the USA. It now becomes a real juggling act to work across the three dimensions of product, country and customer.

The first step is to make a table of the information available. This will enable any gaps to be located and will also focus thought on to resolving the potential conflicts between the different rates.

Table 5.2

Country	Type	Language	Simulation
UK	Private	+ 30% – 10%	+ 120% – 10%
	Corporate	+ 30%	+ 120%
France	Private	+ 15% – 10%	+ 60% – 10%
	Corporate	+ 15%	+ 60%
USA	Private	+ 30% – 5%	+ 120% – 5%
	Corporate	+ 30%	+ 120%
Japan	Private	–	–
	Corporate	+ 15%	+ 60%
Australia	Private	–	–
	Corporate	+ 30%	+120%

Having completed the table, there are enough growth rates to carry out any desired analyses, but it is not clear what should be done in situations where more than one rate is applicable. For example, in the case of sales of the language to private customers in France, two rates apply. First, the overall growth rate for language sales applies (albeit halved in the case of France), but then there is also the estimate that personal sales will decline by 10 per cent there. What rate, or combination, should be used? Unfortunately, there is no one correct answer – it will depend on how the growth rates were first derived. Again it is a case of not applying arithmetic processes without first thinking about the reasons behind them.

Derivation and reliability of growth rates

Although growth rates can be derived from market research or various other forecasting methods, they are much more commonly based on managers' hunches or are selected to look 'reasonable'. If this is the basis of growth rates used in a model, then care needs to be exercised in making decisions based on its results.

Growth rates, however they are derived, are a simplification. Indeed, therein lies much of their attraction. They express in one figure the combined effects of a multitude of complicated interactions. For example, the demand for a firm's product might be affected by their price, their competitors' prices, consumer tastes, the availability of substitute products and so on. As these factors change, so will the demand for the product. A growth rate does not give that information on causation; all it says is that demand changed by x per cent. This makes it a dangerous tool to apply blindly.

Techniques such as multiple regression analysis exist for combining the effect of each determinant of demand into a single growth rate. As already noted though, these techniques tend to be complicated and require significant amounts of data to drive them. However, even if growth rates have been estimated more simply (such as by guessing), it is important to think about the sort of factors that influence demand. A few of the most significant are reviewed next.

Entry into the market

In competitive markets, entry into markets where firms are making reasonable profits will occur unless there are some special sets of conditions to stop them. These special conditions are known as *barriers to entry*. Entry into a market may come from firms not already in the market merging with, or taking over, an existing firm or launching their own product unilaterally. It may also come from firms already in the market differentiating their own products. Barriers to entry are of two main types:

- absolute
- profit-reducing.

Absolute barriers mean that entry is not possible at any cost. Examples of these are rare, but include regulated monopolies, such as the National Grid. Profit-reducing barriers mean that there is a high cost of entry into the market. This will reduce the profitability of being in that market, possibly to the extent that entry becomes unattractive. Profit-reducing barriers to entry include:

- *cost efficiency barriers* either where the existing firms are large and achieving economies of scale or are highly efficient as a result of their experience of the market. This means that the new entrant has two options:

  – compete on non-price terms, perhaps by means of product differentiation
  – incur large losses until volume is high enough or experience great enough to gain similar economies
- *skill barriers* these may be in the form of specific technology skills embodied in patents, people or assets unique to one firm
- *market preference barriers* these may result from factors such as one company setting the standards for micro-computer processors or from established preferences for particular brands.

Both absolute and profit-reducing barriers may be either an institutional feature of the market or specifically erected by a firm wishing to prevent entry to a market. In the case of absolute barriers, this may take the form of lobbying to government, while in the case of profit-reducing barriers, the existing firms may set a price so that it is uneconomic for new firms to enter the market.

In many instances, growth rates are derived with little or no consideration being given to new firms entering the market. When forecasts are made over significant periods of time, this can lead to the model giving highly misleading results.

Product differentiation

The demand for a product or service is influenced by a variety of factors. Particularly in consumer markets, one of the major ones is the differentiation between products. This differentiation may be actual, for example a better level of customer service, or merely an impression created by careful branding, for example that coffee x is better than a supermarket's own brand, even though they are manufactured by the same company to virtually identical specifications.

This is fairly basic stuff, but it is important to mention product differentiation for two reasons. First, because differentiation involves a cost – in advertising and, potentially, in making a higher quality product or delivering a better service. Importantly, this cost is likely to be a long-term one as it will usually be difficult to reduce quality or to change a brand's market positioning

The second important feature of product differentiation is that the advantage it offers is subject to various trends in the market-place, such as fads and fashions. A successful product differentiation will rapidly be mimicked by competitors, unless it can be protected in some way, for example by patents. Therefore, the only advantage available to a firm that successfully differentiates, but cannot protect itself from competitors copying its idea, is time. It is important to build this factor into growth rates.

Product life cycle

Given the complexities of estimating demand referred to above, there have been various attempts to simplify the forecasting process. One of these is known as the product life cycle theory. This states that the demand for a product will vary in a predetermined way over time as it 'ages'. Figure 5.1 shows this as a curve split into four stages: launch, growth, maturity and decline.

The logic of the theory is that, after its launch, the sales of a new product will grow (supposing, of course, that the product is successful), slowly at first and then more rapidly as more people hear about it and, perhaps, its price falls due to improved efficiency. This growth will eventually level off and then, as tastes change, sales will decline.

The theory can provide useful guidance about how demand for a product might be expected to move. In particular, if demand is forecast as a series of

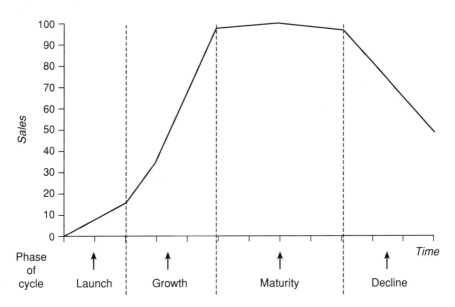

Figure 5.1 The product life cycle curve.

annual growth rates, the model can be used as an alternative to the assumption of linear year on year growth.

Nevertheless, it can also be criticized on a number of grounds. It does not, for example, say *when* any part of the cycle will occur or even if it will. The Mars Bar is often quoted as an example of a product that has never gone into serious decline. The theory does not give any idea of scale, such as how much greater demand can be expected to be in maturity than midway through its growth. In addition to these difficulties, the demand for a product can be thrown off the life cycle course by a number of outside events, such as technological obsolescence and rapid changes in tastes. The product's life may also be prolonged by tactics such as minor design changes, as seen in the car industry, relaunches, retargeting to a different market, such as in the case of the use of aspirin as a drug to reduce blood pressure as well as alleviate headaches, and by expanding sales overseas, particularly to less advanced countries.

Interdependence between firms

The issue of competitors' reactions is vitally important to financial modelling and yet is frequently ignored. As well as interdependence in terms of reacting to product differentiation, firms' pricing decisions are often closely linked. The nature of this linkage is determined, to a large degree, by the market structure. Nevertheless, economic theory is not particularly useful in telling us which of a number of potential options is most likely to occur in any given situation.

Economists are fairly clear that interdependence between firms will be greatest when there are few players in the market. For example, if four firms each have 25 per cent market share and one firm drops its prices to gain a greater share, the sales of its three competitors will fall. They must, therefore, drop their prices, too. The trouble for the firms then is that all their profits have dropped. There is, thus, an incentive to collude with each other and *raise* prices. Collusion is, however, normally illegal and so, instead, the firms must put considerable effort into trying to predict what their competitors will do next. If it is assumed that competition is based solely on price, the consequences of this situation are twofold: continual uncertainty and a tendency for prices to remain fairly 'sticky'.

In reality, price is not the only form of competition and situations of this kind are actually highly unstable as there is always the incentive for firms to break away and so realize greater profits. Product differentiation is one of the main ways of achieving this. However, there will always be a tendency for copycat following. For example, in the washing machine soap market, until recently, there was only one choice – powder. Liquids followed, then, as each firm introduced liquids, concentrated powder, concentrated liquid, non-bleaching powder and so on appeared. Although brands occupied niches, such as Surf being lower priced, differentiation did not, on the whole, allow any firm to break away from interdependence on the others.

Another way of attempting to break away from uncertainty, but not from interdependence, is the establishment of a price leader. This is where one firm, perhaps the largest or most innovative, effectively sets the price for the others. There are three variants of price leadership that are commonly seen:

- *dominant firm leadership* in this case, it is assumed that there is one large firm and a number of small firms and the large one decides what the price should be and the small ones follow, but this is an inherently unstable situation as there is an incentive for a large, low-cost producer to instigate a price war and force the competition out of the market or there is an incentive for the small firms to merge, wield more power and, perhaps, gain economies of scale, so reducing their costs
- *collusion* either by explicit or implicit agreement firms may decide that it is in their joint interests to keep prices in line with each other
- *barometric leadership* barometric price leaders tend to be one of the smaller firms in an industry, this firm being held in high esteem by the others as an efficient and perceptive producer that can be relied on to spot market trends and so guide the other firms.

THE OPERATING COST MODULE

Modelling costs

The logic that is used to manipulate operating costs is very similar to that discussed above for revenue – growth rates are applied to historic figures to give forecasts. There are a number of important differences between the nature of revenue and operating costs, however, that affect how they can be treated in a model.

The first difference concerns the degree of control the firm has over costs and revenues. Clearly, one of the firm's main objectives will be to influence its revenue. However, while it has a number of tools at its disposal to do this (such as advertising, product development, service quality and so on), there are also many factors, external to the firm, that may mitigate the impact of what the firm is trying to do. For example, however much a firm might spend advertising manual typewriters, the development of word processors means that such expenditure would have little impact on demand. In the case of costs, the firm has, in general terms, a much greater degree of control. For example, if the firm decides to reduce overmanning in the accounts department, it can do so (union or staff pressure expecting) by making redundancies.

Operating costs also differ from revenue because at least some proportion of costs is directly related to output or activity. For example, the cost of materials will inevitably rise as more is produced. The important question here concerns how costs and activity are related.

Thus, although there are some costs that are genuinely unknown by the firm (for example, new legislation might be passed affecting emissions to the air), it is usually easier to model the relationship between costs and cost drivers than it is between revenue and revenue drivers. The use of growth rates to describe cost behaviour is, therefore, only part of the story.

The exact form of the operating cost module will vary between models. For example, a road maintenance firm will be concerned about, among other things, the amount of overtime required for manual labour, while a transport company's main focus will be on fuel costs and vehicle maintenance; a high street bank will be interested in the number of transactions made by different types of customer. The discussion here will, therefore, not attempt to present a universal methodology to design the cost module logic, but will focus instead on a few specific issues of relevance to most models.

Fixed costs

All businesses have fixed costs of some sort, but in some the ratio of fixed costs to total costs will be much higher than others. For these businesses, a comparatively small downturn in sales could be disastrous. Financial models will often be employed to try and quantify this risk.

The main rule regarding building fixed costs into a model is to be clear about the costs that really *are* fixed or, perhaps more realistically, within which boundaries costs are fixed. Fixed costs can be defined for modelling purposes as *those costs that show no link to any other variables within the model, when those variables are within anticipated bounds.* This means that costs seen as fixed for management accounting purposes may not be fixed for financial modelling purposes. This is because of the long time periods that models tend to span. For example, the rent for office accommodation is a fixed cost for a financial model *only* if the level of business is not expected to increase so much that further offices are required. If there is the possibility that further office space might be required, then the cost function in the model should incorporate the following kind of relationship:

if office staff < = 200
then office costs = £25 000 per annum
else office costs = £35 000 per annum

In the model itself, these parameters should be clearly laid out in the data section, *not* modelled as:

@if(A21<=200,25 000,35 000)

Instead, the data section might look like this (input numbers are shown bold and formula are displayed).

Table 5.3

	A	B	C
19	Office staff	**215**	
20			
21	OFFICE COSTS		
22	If office staff <=	**200**	**£25 000**
23	If office staff >	+ B22	**£35 000**

The logic section would then have a formula such as:

@if(B19<=B22,C22,C23)

Variable costs

The distinction between fixed and variable costs can be rather fuzzy. The question is really one of degree. In financial modelling terms, variable costs are those costs that are expected to be influenced by changes in other variables within the model.

The nature of the relationship between costs and the variables that influence them – *cost drivers* – is the crucial part of the cost model. Traditional economics assumes that variable costs are related to the level of output. This is often true (for example, raw materials in a manufacturing firm are related to output in this way) and in other cases it may still be a good approximation. None the less, to link all variable costs to output may produce a model that gives a misleading picture of the true behaviour of a system.

In some cases, particularly in service industries, even if costs are genuinely related to output, the relationship is often still hard to quantify because it is difficult to define the output of such organizations. For example, what is the output of a management consultancy, or a research agency? In the consultancy's case, the output could be said to be any of a number of things, such as a completed report, a happy client, increased client efficiency/profitability, staff time spent on analysis and so on. The research agency might share many of these possible outputs and may also include such things as a new patent, a working model or some new discovery. Choosing the right measure to link costs to could, therefore, prove difficult – particularly as the measure most appropriate for performance measurement, in place of the more traditional units sold figure, might be completely inappropriate for modelling.

Led by work in the field of management accounting, attention is now increasingly being turned to associating the level of costs with a much wider range of cost drivers. The objective of this is to associate only appropiate costs with an activity.

Activity-based costing (ABC) works in this way via a four-stage process:

- *identify and cost activities* an activity is something that resources, primarily people or assets, are dedicated to, for example, in a supermarket, activities include stacking shelves, checkout operation, cashing up, stock-taking and so on, and activities, typically, are identified and costed by means of a series of interviews
- *identify the cost drivers associated with each activity* for example, cost drivers in the supermarket operation will include the volume of customers and the range of products
- *group activities into pools on the basis of common cost drivers* and, consequently, work out a cost per unit of the activity
- *produce costs for individual services or product lines*, this is done by using the unit costs, and the resulting product costs are clearly particularly useful for modelling purposes.

Points to remember

At least four important points come out of all this. First, modellers need to take great care when using cost data from traditional accounting systems where that data includes allocations of overhead. For example, to accept that a product cost is, say, £1.31, where £0.77 is the direct cost of production and £0.54 is the allocated overhead, and then to use that cost to project forward could give rise to completely wrong conclusions. This is because the allocation of overhead may bear no relationship to the level of activity and, therefore, as volume rises, the product cost may not move in a realistic manner. Second, financial models should take account of appropriate cost drivers whenever practical. Third, models must be aware of the range within which their estimates of short-run cost relationships are valid. For example, a product cost will be based on a particular service delivery or product production, set-up. Eventually, though, some level of capacity will be reached that will require a new set-up and so product costs may alter. Fourth, models should consider the form of the cost driver–cost relationship. Is it linear, stepped, curved or does it take some other form?

This last point about the nature of the cost function is particularly important. As an example, consider staff costs. A simplified staff cost calculation might calculate the total of standard and overtime pay to give total pay. The standard pay component of the calculation is straightforward enough as the pay of each employee will be known and can be summed to give the total pay for the year. The overtime pay element is potentially more complicated. This is because the amount of overtime worked will be a function of factors such as output, efficiency and capacity. Output affects overtime because if the workforce is unchanged and the same ratio of input to output is produced, then overtime may need to rise to increase output. Efficiency affects overtime levels because if less input can produce the same output, then less overtime will be required. Capacity affects overtime because if there is spare capacity, overtime may not be required.

Formulating a relationship to link staff cost to all these elements is potentially quite a complicated task. One thing is certain, though, whatever relationship is decided on, it with will not be linear. Putting some figures to the above example will illustrate this. Using the above figures to do some cost calculations, the following information is produced.

EXAMPLE **The base data (Last year's figures).**

Average production staff	300 full-time equivalent staff
Standard weekly hours	40 hours, less 5 hours for paid breaks
Standard week	5 days
Average output	0.8 units per person per hour
Working days in year	230 days
Standard rate	£3.80 per hour

Overtime rate	£5.70 per hour
Redundancy cost	£2000 per person
Total output for last year	438 442 units

Using the above figures to do some cost calculations, the following information is produced.

Units produced at standard rate	$= 300 \times (40\text{--}5)/5 \times 0.8 \times 230$
	$= 386\ 400$ units per annum
Units produced at overtime rate	$= 438\ 442 - 386\ 400$
	$= 52\ 042$ units per annum
Overtime worked	$= 52\ 042/0.8$
	$= 65\ 052$ hours
Total standard pay	$= 300 \times 40 \times 52 \times £3.80$
	$= £2\ 371\ 200$ per annum
Total overtime pay	$= 65.052 \times £5.70$
	$= £370\ 799.25$ per annum
Total pay	$= £2\ 741\ 999.25$ per annum

It is forecast that efficiency will improve next year from 0.8 to 0.95 units per hour.

To produce the same output, only 287 staff would be required and no overtime. Assuming that the surplus 13 staff were made redundant, but that the remaining staff were given a pay rise of 5 per cent, then the staff cost for next year would be as follows.

Total standard pay	$= 287 \times 40 \times 52 \times (£3.80 \times 1.05)$
	$= £2\ 381\ 870$ per annum
Redundancy costs	$= 13 \times £2000$
	$= £26\ 000$
Total staff cost	$= £2\ 407\ 870.40$

Calculating staff costs per unit of output produces the following figures.

Last year	£6.25 per unit
This year	£5.49 per unit (including redundancy costs)
	£5.43 per unit (excluding redundancy costs)

Therefore, an 18.75 per cent rise in efficiency has decreased unit staff costs by 12.2 per cent if redundancy costs are included or 13.1 per cent if they are not. There are two reasons why costs have fallen by less than the efficiency rise:

- a 5 per cent pay rise was given to the remaining workers – if this and the redundancy costs had been excluded, then the reduction in unit staff costs would have been 17.3 per cent
- there is now some spare capacity – 287 staff could produce 438 966 units, that is, 524 more than they did.

This example shows why it is important to build costs up from non-financial data, such as numbers of people, whenever possible. This will allow changes and different scenarios to be run. If this had not been done and only the actual costs had been modelled, then it would have been necessary to somehow derive the (non-linear) relationship between efficiency, pay rates, output, capacity and total staff mathematically for the model to be accurate – clearly a much more difficult task. In reality, though, it would have been more likely that some simplified relationship would have been used, so losing important information.

Before moving on from variable costs, it is worth noting the potential relationship between operating costs and capital expenditure. For example, the purchase of a new machine could change efficiency, materials use, staffing requirements and a whole host of other variables. This seems obvious, but it sometimes easy to forget the need to model all these effects.

THE WORKING CAPITAL MODULE

Cash flow analysis is usually important in financial modelling because the economic viability of a project or proposed action is best evaluated on the basis of the cash (not accounting profit) returns that are made on the investment. However, much of the information available to the financial modeller, such as sales and purchases, comes from the accounting system. This means that accruals-based data from the accounting systems must be translated into cash flow data for use by the model. The working capital module is concerned with this difference between cash and accruals data.

To illustrate the nature of working capital, consider a firm of architects undertaking a number of projects, each of which lasts several months. During a project, they will incur costs (staff time, use of computers, travel and so on), but they can only bill their client when the work is complete. As far as their profit and loss account is concerned, if the work has been carried out, then both the costs incurred during that time and some portion of the eventual revenue will be attributed to that period, even though the revenue has not yet been received. For cash flow purposes, the costs are incurred in that period and, therefore, are part of the cash flow. However, the revenue has not yet been received and so it is not a cash flow item. Cash flow and profit and loss account are therefore different. This difference is due to working capital.

Working capital can be one of four main types:

- debtors,
- creditors,
- work in progress (WIP)
- stock.

There are two main ways in which a model can take account of working capital. It can use different revenue and cost figures between the cash flow and the profit and loss account to allow for the differences. Alternatively, it can use the same figures in both and simply make an adjustment for the movement in working capital in the cash flow. The latter is the most common approach.

In modelling working capital, it is useful to think of it in terms of days – the number of days it takes debtors to pay, the number of days' credit the firm takes before paying, the number of days' stock held and so on. In the first year of operation, there will be an initial build-up of working capital. In subsequent years, changes will occur either when the number of creditor, debtor or stock days changes, or when sales or purchases change. As working capital will ultimately require to be financed, care must be taken to estimate the requirement for capital in money of the day (that is, inflated) prices. If this is not done and a bank facility is taken out to cover the requirement, there might be inadequate funds.

Calculating the change in working capital involves two stages. The first requirement is for calculating total stock, total debtors and total creditors, then calculating the increase (or decrease over last year). The total figures are calculated by taking, for example, the number of days' stock divided by 365 days and multiplying that number by (in the case of stock) raw material purchases in the period. The increase in stock plus the increase in debtors less the increase in creditors then gives the increase in working capital that must be financed. The example that follows shows this more clearly.

EXAMPLE The profit and loss account figures are as follows.

	1996	*1997*	*1998*
Unit sales	5000	6000	8000
Price	£270	£280	£290
Revenue	£1.35m	£1.68m	£2.32m
Operating costs	£0.50m	£0.60m	£0.75m

The working capital analysis shows that, debtors are expected to pay in an average of 19 days, that 25 day's credit is taken, on average, and that there is not WIP. Thus, the following figures were calculated.

	1996	1997	1998
Total debtors	19/365 × £1.35m = £70 274	19/365 × £1.68m = £87 452	19/365 × £2.32m = £120 767
Total creditors	25/365 × £0.50m = £34 247	25/365 × £0.60m = £41 096	25/365 × £0.75m = £51 370
Net increase in working capital	£70 274–£34 247 = £36 027	(£87 452–£70 274) –(£41 096–£34 247) = £10 329	(£120 767–£87 452) –(£51 370–£41 096) = £23 041

CAPITAL COST MODULE

Capital costs are items of expenditure that provide a stream of benefits lasting longer than one year and, therefore, must be depreciated for accounting purposes. They appear on the balance sheet at original cost less accumulated depreciation, that is, at their *written down* value. For modelling purposes, capital costs are usually very straightforward. They will appear in the cash flow in the year the money is spent and, if a profit and loss account and balance sheet are part of the model, they will appear there as depreciation and written down asset values. The capital cost module, therefore, is essentially a list of expenditure phased over time.

Complexity, such as there is, arises from the need to split expenditure to take account of factors such as the following.

- Extended payment terms, where for example, a machine is bought (when the contract was signed) and delivered in May 1995, but payment is split so that 25 per cent is paid on delivery, then a further 25 per cent in 3, 6 and 9 months' time. In this case, the total cost of the machine will appear in the balance sheet as soon as it is delivered, but the cash flow will show the staggered payments.
- Different types of capital expenditure will be depreciated in different ways. For example computers might be depreciated straight line (see under Depreciation below) over three years, cars by the reducing balance method over four years and so on. Depreciation will be looked at under the fixed assets module, but for now it is important to note that different

types of expenditure must be split and held separately in this module so that they can then feed into the asset module.

- The tax calculation will also need to take an input from capital expenditure because various allowances against tax are available for capital expenditure. Again, this will necessitate that a split be made in the capital expenditure module so that appropriate values can be passed to the tax module.

THE FIXED ASSET MODULE

Fixed, or capital, assets must be recorded and shown at their written down value in the balance sheet. The depreciation charge for the year must also be shown in the profit and loss account. Fixed assets and depreciation are, however, of little or no relevance to NPV-based financial analysis as it is conducted on a cash basis. Nevertheless, many financial models do output full financial statements and, therefore, need to deal with assets and depreciation. Even if they do not, then the same information may be required to calculate performance measures, such as ROCE.

There are, therefore, two functions of this module. First, a score-keeping function – it records the cost of assets and subtracts their depreciation. Its second function is to calculate depreciation and the entries associated with the disposal of assets. The score-keeping functions are quite straightforward as, essentially, they are lists of assets. The calculation functions are briefly examined below.

Depreciation

There are several types of depreciation in use, the most common being the straight line method, which means that an equal amount of depreciation is charged each period over the life of the asset. The most popular alternative method, which weights charges toward the early years of an asset's life, is called the reducing balance method.

For financial modelling purposes, assets are normally most conveniently held as a 'pool'. For example, all machinery is added together and manipulated as a single figure. The same happens with computers, vehicles, buildings and so on. A depreciation charge is then applied to the whole pool. Thus, if the purchase cost of the pool is £3 million and the depreciation method is straight line over 10 years, then, assuming that the assets have no scrap value at the end of their life, the annual depreciation charge would be £300 000.

The use of this method involves keeping three basic pieces of information about the assets in the pool: purchase cost, annual depreciation charge and accumulated depreciation. This will enable the written down value (that is, cost less accumulated depreciation) to be calculated. All assets in one pool must use the same depreciation rate and method. A complexity may arise in when it comes to the disposal of assets and this is looked at in the next section.

In the case of start-up projects or where the remaining lives of assets are known, it is a simple task to remove assets from the pool once they are fully depreciated. If, for example, the life of assets is five years, then, after five years, the purchase cost of assets from five years ago should be subtracted from the current purchase cost and, similarly for accumulated depreciation. If there is a mix of assets existing at the start of the project and assets that will be purchased during the project, then a separate schedule will be required to tell the model when to drop existing assets from the pool. An example of a simple calculation follows, with straight line depreciation over three years.

Table 5.4

	Year				
	1994	*1995*	*1996*	*1997*	*1998*
Historic cost B/fwd.	0	107	595	686	828
Capital expenditure	107	488	91	249	433
Losses from pool	0	0	0	107	488
Historic cost C/fwd	107	595	686	828	773
Depreciation charge in period	0	36	198	229	276
Cumulative depreciation	0	36	234	356	144
Written down value	107	559	452	472	629

In this example, no depreciation is charged in the year of purchase; but this is not always the case.

Disposal of assets

A problem with not maintaining individual records of assets can arise when assets are disposed of. When an asset is disposed of, three entries are required in the model:

- its net book value (purchase cost less accumulated depreciation) must be cleared from the balance sheet
- the cash from the sale must be added in to the cash flow
- the profit (or loss) on its disposal (that is, the cash received less the net book value) must be charged to the profit and loss account.

In order to do this, it is necessary to have records of the purchase cost and accumulated depreciation for the individual asset, but recording assets in a pool hides this information. If charges on disposals are likely to be important, then assets that are to be disposed of later in the model must be held individually. Obviously, this will add to the size of the model.

THE TAXATION MODULE

Taxation is a complicated subject. Individual projects or strategies can create quite intricate tax effects, particularly in a situation where a group of companies is involved or when profits are earned in various different countries. However, taxation is a fairly unavoidable cost of being successful in business and, thus, making a profit. Financial models, therefore, often wish to estimate the tax impacts of a project.

Detailed taxation calculations are covered in a number of regularly updated, and widely obtainable manuals. Therefore, the discussion here will be confined to a brief overview[1] of some of the central aspects of company tax for modelling purposes, that is:

- basic UK corporation tax calculation
- advance corporation tax (ACT)
- basic considerations in a group situation.

Basic corporation tax calculation

The major UK company tax is corporation tax (CT). In the tax year 1993/94, the basic CT rate was 33 per cent of 'chargeable profits' for large companies. CT is due nine months in arrears. Chargeable profits for CT are not the same as the profit declared in the profit and loss account. Therefore, the calculation of chargeable profit is the first step in the CT calculation. Profit before tax forms the starting point for the calculation. A number of adjustments are made to this figure to arrive at chargeable profits. First, items that are charged to accounting profits, but are disallowable for tax purposes, are added back. These include:

- accounting depreciation
- general provisions
- capital expenditure.

Second, a number of deductions are made, which include:

- capital allowances
- certain losses
- certain loan interest paid.

Capital allowances

Standard accounting depreciation is not allowed as a deduction for tax purposes in the UK. The reason for this is primarily that depreciation policy is under the control of the company and, therefore, if it were an allowable deduction, each company could select a depreciation policy so as to minimize its tax liability. A set of capital allowances are available instead. These are not available on all capital expenditure, though, and their rates are predefined.

The two major categories of capital allowance that *are* available are for industrial buildings and plant and machinery. Industrial buildings – which can vary from a factory to a toll road to a hotel – are eligible for an allowance of 4 per cent of their cost each year over 25 years. In the case of plant and machinery, a 25 per cent writing down allowance (WDA) is available on the (allowable) cost of the asset. This means that if an asset cost £1000, then the WDA in the first year would be £1000 × 0.25 = £250, (£1000 – £250) × 0.25 = £187.50 in the second year, and so on.

Losses

If a company makes a loss (that is, a negative chargeable profit) in any year, it does not have to pay any CT. It can carry this loss forward, to be set off against future (positive) chargeable profits, for an indefinite period. Thus if a company had a loss of £100 last year, but made a profit of £75 in the current year, then the chargeable profit for the year will be £75 – £100 = – £25. Therefore, no tax will be paid and £25 of unused losses can be carried forward to use against future trading profits. Losses may also be set against profits of the preceding three years.

Loan interest

Interest on loans, which includes debenture interest and bank loans, is normally allowable as a deduction against chargeable profit. Overdraft interest is normally also deductible.

Advance corporation tax

When a company pays a dividend, it must pay a proportion of its CT charge for that period at the same time. The amount payable is called advance corporation tax (ACT). If d is the net dividend paid and t the rate of ACT, then ACT is calculated as:

$$\text{ACT} = d \left(\frac{t}{100 - t} \right)$$

Therefore, if chargeable profit is £1000 and £775 is paid as dividend during the 1993 fiscal year, then:

$$\begin{aligned} \text{ACT} &= £775 \times 22.5/77.5 \\ &= £225 \end{aligned}$$

The 'mainstream' CT bill (which will be paid later) is then reduced by this amount, subject to a maximum reduction:

Mainstream CT   = £1000 × 33 per cent
                = £330
less ACT of £225   = £75

If the ACT payment exceeds the maximum set-off allowed, then the 'surplus ACT' can be set off against CT liabilities over the last six years. If there is still insufficient liability to utilize the surplus ACT, it may be carried forward indefinitely or it can be surrendered (used by) a subsidiary company to offset against their own CT liability.

Group tax

The surrender of surplus ACT is one example of the tax impact of groups of companies. Another example is that tax losses can be transferred within a UK group of companies. For these purposes a 'group' is a UK parent company and all UK subsidiaries in which it has a 75 per cent or greater stake. The modeller should be aware that these provisions exist, but again, as the legislation is complicated, professional tax assistance should be sought.

THE FINANCING MODULE

Almost every project needs to be financed in some way, be it from a bank overdraft, retained earnings or a complicated mix of debt and equity issued specifically to finance the project. Modelling finance can be quite involved, so this section briefly reviews some of the main issues and suggests possible solutions.

Issues in modelling financing

In the discussion of working capital it was said that most models are concerned primarily with cash flow analysis. This observation is important when looking at finance because the need for financing is dictated by cash needs, not accounting profits or losses. Considerable effort, therefore, is often put into exploring different financing structures. Usually, the main objective is to allocate the risk and reward components of a project among different types of lender and/or investor so that enough people can be provided with an adequate risk–return relationship for the financing to go ahead. Achieving this may require the use of any number of the hundreds of financial instruments, such as loans (syndicated, senior, subordinated, overdraft, secured, unsecured and so on), commercial paper, floating rate notes, leases, eurobonds, options, warrants, convertibles and so on.

The splitting of the project returns among a number of financing instruments can be nothing short of a nightmare for the financial modeller. Consider the following example, which is a version of a real life project financing.

EXAMPLE A project is to be financed by a mix of equity, a syndicated bank loan and a cheap-rate loan from the European Bank. In addition, there is a bank overdraft facility that is used to finance working capital and as a contingency fund in case sales do not materialize as quickly as planned. The covenants on the loan state that the ratio of equity to total debt must be maintained at or above 35 per cent at all times.

The equity and loan will be drawn down as required, subject to maximum limits over a three-year period. A fee will be charged for arranging the loan, calculated as a percentage of the facility made available. A further 'commitment fee' will be charged on the difference between the total facility and the amount already drawn. The interest and fees on the loan during the three-year period will be capitalized, that is, they will be added to the value of the loan outstanding. Loan repayments will be made semi-annually, starting six months after the end of the three-year draw down period.

The European Bank's loan specifies a repayment schedule over 15 years. The syndicated loan is to be repaid at a set percentage of project cash flows calculated after the European Bank's loan has been repaid, but before the overdraft or equity have been paid.

Although this may seem to be quite a complicated example, many of the problems that it poses are, in fact, quite common. The main modelling problem in this example is the requirement to maintain a constant ratio of equity to total debt. Specifically, this presents two difficulties:

- the commitment fee on the loan is calculated as a percentage of the total loan, which itself will include the capitalized fees and interest, less drawings to date (this is what spreadsheet users know as a CIRCular relationship, that is, one variable depends on another that, in its turn depends on the first one)
- the specification tells us what the ratio of equity to total debt should be, but does not fully specify which of the three debt instruments (syndicated loan, European Bank's loan and overdraft facility) should be used to fund what, so some form of decision rule must be programmed to overcome this, for example, draw European and syndicated loan in equal amounts.

Running the model dynamically will throw up further problems. For example, if the construction period is lengthened, interest may have to be capitalized for longer. The model will need to be flexible in allowing the user to switch this, as it will other variables, such as the loan's life and interest/fee rates.

Sensitivity analysis may also make the model 'badly behaved'. For example, if revenues are reduced, net cash flow might become negative. In this case, the overdraft will increase and repayments of the syndicated loan will cease. This would probably not be a realistic picture of reality, though, as the situation would almost certainly breach loan covenants and put the project into default.

Another twist arises from the fact that, as debt is repaid, the equity to total debt ratio will also change, which the model may wish to address by repaying equity or reducing the overdraft. The selection of how to proceed again requires the definition of firm decision rules.

Approaches to modelling financing

Although many people become very bogged down attempting to model financing, it does not need to be that complicated. The CIRCularity problem is common, but it need not be the end of the world. Indeed, it is acceptable to have a CIRCularity in a model – if it converges. That is, if, in the case of a spreadsheet, after calculating several times, the answer stops changing. This will normally be the case with financing CIRCularities. What it means is that relationships can be programmed as they really are and the spreadsheet simply allowed to iterate until a stable answer is reached.

The problem of values depending on themselves can also be solved by thinking of the relationship as a mathematical series. For example, imagine a situation where a loan had to be drawn in order to pay the interest on the loan as well as finance the project. In this case, the loan has to be drawn for the project cost, then a bigger loan is required to cover the interest, but then, because that interest has increased, the loan interest is required on the interest and so on. This forms what is known as a geometric series and there is a simple formula for finding its sum to infinity, which is what is required in this case. If the drawing for capital expenditure is £1000 and the interest is 10 per cent, then £1000/(1–10 per cent) = £1111, which must be drawn to pay the interest as well.

Other problems are usually the result of insufficiently precise decision rules. If, for example, there is more than one type of debt instrument being used, then some rule must be specified that lets the model know which loan to use for what purpose. Then, finally, thought must also be given to the bounds of the model, that is, what happens when parameters vary dramatically. This problem will be returned to in Chapter 9, when model audit and testing are discussed.

Notes

[1] Actual tax calculations are based on a large number of detailed definitions about exactly what assets are allowable for capital allowances, what profit or income losses carried forward can be set off against tax and so on. The discussion here is greatly simplified and is designed to be used in the order to arrive at a 'ball park' tax figure. If tax is an important aspect of a model, then it is essential that detailed professional advice is sought.

Part III

MODEL BUILDING

6

SELECTION OF COMPUTER SYSTEMS

INTRODUCTION

Financial modellers must have a variety of skills: a grasp of economics, abilities in financial evaluation and accounting and maybe technical skills relevant to their own organization. These skills are all related to the business aspects of their modelling. In addition to these abilities, they must also be adept at working with computers. Much of this skill lies in knowing how to get the best from software and this comes from experience and training. However, it is also necessary to have the right tools for the job in the first place. The hardware and software selected may have a dramatic impact on the quality of the analysis carried out.

Hardware

Financial models can become very complicated, requiring a great number of calculations by the machine. They can also be large, taking up a lot of disk space. They may, depending on the software chosen, also require substantial amounts of memory. These requirements imply a hardware configuration comprising a powerful processor, a reasonably large hard disk and sufficient amounts of memory. As financial models are often influencing documents, they must also look good. This requires that a high-resolution screen and printer be added to the requirements.

Models are developed on a variety of types of hardware ranging from standalone PCs, through departmental midrange systems up to large corporate mainframes. Away from the world of PCs, the processor power, disk and memory size issues are simply a matter of ensuring that sufficient power is made available by the system's manager. Back in the PC arena, storage limitations can be a major problem, which can manifest itself in a number of ways:

- absolute limitations may be put on the size of the model by lack of disk or memory or by insufficient processor power

- lack of power may encourage the development of cramped models that are difficult to read, poorly laid out and, therefore, prone to errors
- models may take a long time to run, so reducing their usefulness in periods of pressure.

It is important, therefore, that PC hardware is adequate for the job. Over recent years, the cost of PC hardware has dropped dramatically as new processors have been introduced that offer greater power at less cost (see Figure 6.1[1]). Hard disk and memory prices have also fallen. The speed of change in the market for PC hardware is still rapid. A powerful processor is not the end of the story, though. The speed with which the processor can communicate with the memory, disk and screen all are also critical to the system's overall performance. Financial models of any great complexity can make use of the best hardware available.

Operating environment

When a particular application is run on a computer, the relationship between the application software and the computer hardware (screen, disk, memory

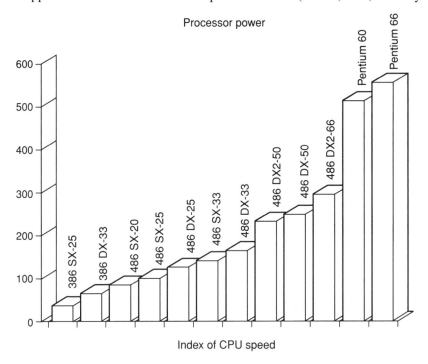

Figure 6.1 Processor power

and so on) is handled by another piece of software known as an operating system. During the 1980s, the most widely used PC operating system was DOS, in one of various versions. In the early 1990s, a new operating system[2], Microsoft Windows, became the standard for new PC purchases. Despite this, DOS still has a massive user base. Nevertheless, some products, such as Microsoft's own spreadsheet, Excel, are only available on Windows. Windows differs from DOS in a number of ways.

- It uses graphical symbols, called icons, on the screen that are selected using a mouse instead of typing commands at the keyboard as in DOS. This makes Windows easier to learn and use than DOS.
- It standardizes printer control so that *all* applications can use *all* the features of any devices for which there is a Windows driver. This contrasts with DOS, which requires different drivers for each program. Therefore, under DOS, spreadsheet x might be able to access printer A's fonts, whereas spreadsheet y could not.
- It allows several applications to be open and running at the same time, that is it *multitasks*. Although the method of multitasking used by Windows is somewhat crude by the standards of midrange systems, nevertheless, it allows different applications (such as word processors, databases and spreadsheets) to exchange and share information much more easily than under DOS. The exact facilities available vary from program to program, but two main standards are supported: object linking and embedding (OLE) and dynamic data exchange (DDE).
- OLE is a facility whereby an 'object', such as a graphic, table or piece of text, can be copied ('embedded') from one application into another. Changes can then be made to the embedded object without leaving the application in which the object has been embedded simply by using the mouse to select the object, which will call up the creating application program to enable changes to be made. Once the changes have been made, the user is returned to the original application to carry on. Apart from ease of use, OLE also offers an efficient use of disk space because objects do not need to be fully replicated in each place they are used.
- DDE is a means of creating a self-updating link between pieces of information, such as tables or graphics, in multiple applications. For example, if a word processed document refers to a table created by a spreadsheet program, a DDE link could be established between the two applications and then whenever the spreadsheet altered, the word processed document would immediately reflect these changes.

Although some users find the use of a graphical interface a slower method of selecting commands than the keyboard, the use of on-screen icons to carry out certain functions can often aid productivity. Even if personal preference mitigates against the use of a graphical interface, the other benefits of Windows, and the fact that software developers appear to view it as the way forward, suggest that Windows is likely to carry on gaining market share.

An alternative operating system for the PC is IBM's OS/2 operating system. OS/2 dispenses with the need for DOS completely, although it will run both DOS and Windows programs. It is widely regarded as a superior product to Windows technically, but, despite this, it has failed to attract a sizeable user base. This is sometimes attributed to poor marketing on IBM's behalf, but is also due to the large base of Windows programs available and the large (30MB or greater) amount of hard disk that OS/2 requires. There is also a complete alternative to PCs: the Apple Macintosh range of computers. In many ways these offer similar benefits to Windows, but (according to their fanatically loyal user base) more so.

Software

The financial modeller has six main software options:

- conventional spreadsheets, such as Microsoft Excel
- traditional financial modelling languages, such as FCS
- multidimensional modelling packages, such as Lotus Improv
- standard computer programming languages, such as COBOL
- database packages, such as DBase IV
- ready-built models, both complete programs and ready-made spreadsheets, such as MBA Business Plan.

It was noted earlier that spreadsheets are far and away the dominant software presently used for financial modelling. Many of the problems facing financial modellers therefore centre on the use of spreadsheets. Because of this, the discussion here will focus on examining the advantages and limitations of spreadsheets. Recent enhancements to the major packages will then be looked at. These discussions will provide a context within which other software options can be examined.

SPREADSHEETS

A typical spreadsheet consists of a number of components:

- a matrix of cells into which numbers, formulae and functions can be entered, which will, normally, consist of either two (rows and columns) or three (rows, columns and sheets/files) dimensions
- operators (commands) to manage cell contents, for example, move, copy, graph, format, and to manage the worksheet itself, such as file, print, quit
- macro language – used to automate processes and to enable a spreadsheet to be used without expert knowledge
- 'add-ons', supplied either by the spreadsheet company or a third party, that add new commands, such as forecasting.

Developments in spreadsheet software

The ease of use and flexibility of spreadsheets have carried them a long way. However, the requirements of users are now also much greater – fuelled by a combination of their early successes and by the availability of more powerful hardware. As demands on the software have grown, so have the problems. Early spreadsheet programs did not allow large models to be built in a structured fashion.

Modern packages have evolved a number of features that are designed to improve models. One of the most significant is the ability to use multiple, linked spreadsheets and/or files, rather than working with all the information on a single sheet. This enables parts of the model to be developed independently and then combined later so that more than one modeller can work on developments at any time. It also means that different parts of the model can be changed without having unwanted side-effects on other parts.

The second advance of spreadsheets is in improved output presentation. A well-presented model can significantly improve understanding of a model's output. The features that contribute towards this better presentation include the ability to use different text styles and sizes, the integration of graphics and features such as lines, boxes and shading into the spreadsheet and much greater control over the printer so that text can be automatically fitted on to one page and headings, footers and so on can be incorporated.

Ease of use has always been a strong point of spreadsheets and, as the medium has developed, this feature has been further enhanced. Features that are now commonplace include automatic labelling of columns with the months of the year, 'undo' facilities that enable mistakes to be corrected and 'scenario managers' that allow the modelling of a variety of different situations to be handled in a structured fashion. Versions of software that run under the Windows operating system tend to offer even more features to improve ease of use, such as the ability to apply predefined formats (or 'style sheets') to a range of cells.

Spreadsheets have also improved in a number of other ways. For example, their computational capability is better as a result of more efficient recalculation routines and better memory management. Linkages to other software packages, external databases and other files on a network are now also possible. Spreadsheet manufacturers can be expected to place increasing emphasis on these links in an aim to lock their products into the wider corporate IT environment.

Advantages and limitations

As noted above, spreadsheets have undergone substantial development since their inception in the late 1970s. None the less, there are many who would contend that they are still an inappropriate tool for all but the simplest of financial modelling tasks. Therefore, it is perhaps worth considering what general features of spreadsheets make them either suitable or unsuitable for financial modelling.

The advantages of spreadsheets have already been referred to. The most apparent of these is the ease with which results can be generated and changes made. There are two reasons for this. First, very little training is needed to begin to use a spreadsheet and, second, because spreadsheets come with many facilities already built in, there is very little preparatory 'programming' required before outputs are obtained. For example, printing is simply a matter of selecting an area and pressing the 'go' key – there is no need to specify which portion of the output should be printed at which location on the page because the layout is already defined by the spreadsheet. Spreadsheets are also very good at presentation: sophisticated graphing facilities are included as standard and fonts and other formatting commands are easily changed.

Many of the failings of spreadsheets are consequences of the same features that make them easy to use. For example, the ability to place data or text or formulae anywhere on the sheet means that the modeller is not limited in how to lay out the model. However, it *also* means that data and formulae can become mixed together, making it difficult at times to spot which are data and which are formulae, and that there are no standard ways of laying out a model, making it more difficult for people who have not been involved in its construction to understand its operation.

The lack of structure inherent in spreadsheets means that they can be difficult to navigate around unless some 'map' of the location of different entries is produced. Spreadsheets are also often difficult to audit because the relationships contained in formulae may be complicated, referring to cells dispersed around the model, making the tracking down of errors difficult. Spreadsheets also cause problems for data security because it is difficult to prevent data or logic being changed by unauthorized users.

The most modern spreadsheets overcome a lot of these problems, but they do so at a cost. In common with a lot of more recent software they require substantial processor power, large amounts of memory, considerable hard disk space and often quite high-resolution graphics. All these requirements are expensive, despite the fall in the price of processor power and memory over recent years. They also act as a barrier to users with older hardware as, to upgrade to new versions of the software, they also need to invest in more powerful hardware.

Whether or not the sum of these arguments is seen to favour spreadsheets over a programming or modelling language is, to some degree, a matter of individual preference. None the less, as the price of computing power falls and the functionality of spreadsheets rises, the spreadsheet format seems likely to retain its dominance. The multidimensional analysis capabilities of products such as Lotus Improv and CA Compete! (see below) are now migrating into mainstream spreadsheet products. This represents another substantial movement forward in spreadsheet power.

The selection of packages

There are many spreadsheet packages on the market, but a only relatively small number have significant market share. The best-known is Lotus 123. Many of the cheaper packages are really clones of Lotus. Other important packages are Microsoft's Excel, Computer Associate's Supercalc and Borland's Quattro Pro. The situation is complicated by the fact that all of these packages have been through a number of incarnations and so, consequently, there are many different versions in use, sometimes with dramatically differing functionality. In some cases, there are multiple versions of software actively being marketed at one time. Thus, at the beginning of 1993, Lotus 123 had 5 versions: a basic version (version 2.4) for IBM-compatible PCs running the DOS operating system, a more complicated version (version 3.1+), again for PCs and DOS, an Apple Macintosh version, a version for PCs running the Windows operating system *and* a version for OS/2.

Deciding which spreadsheet package to use will be governed by a variety of factors. These include:

- *corporate software policy* it is increasingly likely that any corporate IT function will seek to standardize on a particular product or the products of one vendor in order to reduce training costs, make support easier and to gain bulk discounts and, if this is the case, the selection has already been made
- *familiarity* when a company or department has been using a particular product for some time, it can make sense to stay with that product through its updates because the learning curve staff must go through will be less steep, but some packages try to ease the transition from a competitor product to their own by offering file and/or command compatibility
- *operating system* the choice between DOS, Windows, OS/2 and Apple Macintosh operating environments may limit choice, for example, Excel is not available for DOS
- *unique features* although the major products offer quite similar levels of functionality, there are still features offered by one package not available on others, and these may prove decisive for particular applications
- *links to other software* it is becoming increasingly important for different applications to transfer data between each other, for example, spreadsheet tables and graphs need to be easily pulled into word processed documents and spreadsheets running on PCs need to access corporate data, which may be held on midrange and mainframe systems, and different software products offer varying degrees of compatibility with other software.

NON-SPREADSHEET SOFTWARE OPTIONS

Traditional modelling languages

Before the advent of PCs and spreadsheets, most financial modelling was carried out on corporate mainframes using either one of a number of software packages designed for the purpose or one produced by bespoke programming. Some of the packages used then still exist and have migrated to the PC world. Two of the better known are FCS and EVA Mini. They are mainly used for large, complicated models – particularly those that have to access big volumes of data or models that are to become institutionalized into the corporate software environment, perhaps for an application such as budgeting.

These packages are inherently inflexible because they involve programming the model in a similar fashion to a language such as BASIC. This makes their usefulness to most financial modelling applications highly questionable, as financial models tend to evolve as new problems are found or answers arrived at. The age and mainframe heritage of these packages also mean that their presentational capabilities are limited. On the plus side, though, they are better than spreadsheets in their handling of data because they separate data storage and manipulation functions from analysis functions.

On balance, this approach may be useful for models that need to access and manipulate large amounts of data, but only when the model logic can be well-specified in advance, when that logic will undergo little change over the model's life and when sophisticated graphical presentation is not required.

Multi-dimensional modelling packages

This is a comparatively new category of product that has been developed in an attempt to overcome the limitations of traditional spreadsheets. The two main examples are Lotus Improv and Computer Associates Compete!. They are based on a spreadsheet format, but offer database-like capabilities to manipulate information. They do this by offering the user the ability to select different 'views' of the data.

To illustrate this consider Table 6.1, which is an extract from the sales database of a fictional management consultancy.

If this data were entered into a spreadsheet in its current form, spreadsheet analysis would be cumbersome because of the two (row and column) or three (row, column and sheet/file) dimensional nature of spreadsheets. For example, if an analysis of regional sales, split by division and product were required, a spreadsheet would have to either use unwieldy data extract commands or reorganize the table into a more appropriate format. Although some spreadsheet packages do improve on this position by offering a cross-tabulation tool (the Crosstab Wizard in Excel, version 4 and later), using Compete! or Improv, the same table can be produced with a few simple mouse commands.

These packages do make the initial set-up of models more complicated, as they take away some of a spreadsheet's free formatting capability. However, this has the benefit of imposing discipline on the modeller and can be a useful prompt for thought before programming begins. Their ease of use is otherwise good, as is their presentational capability (although still lagging somewhat behind the best spreadsheets). This software can be recommended, in preference to spreadsheets or modelling languages, for complicated models that need to work with large volumes of multidimensional data.

Table 6.1

Sales database

Month	Product	Region	Division	Revenue
January	Review	South	Strategy	£105 089
October	Market study	Scotland	Strategy	£56 363
September	Implementation	South	IT	£130 175
April	Market study	Wales	Strategy	£222 031
April	IT strategy	South	IT	£294 169
February	Review	South	Strategy	£62 873
November	Review	North	Strategy	£353 505
September	Review	North	Strategy	£108 164
July	IT strategy	Scotland	IT	£521 042
July	Review	London	Strategy	£36 527
March	BS 5750	North	BPI	£32 035
March	BS 5750	Wales	BPI	£6 536
May	Review	Wales	Strategy	£490 643
March	IT strategy	Scotland	IT	£82 402
July	BS 5750	Scotland	BPI	£402 894
January	Implementation	London	IT	£289 091
December	Market study	Scotland	Strategy	£730 854
December	IT strategy	London	IT	£118 646
October	Market study	North	Strategy	£521 047
November	Market study	Scotland	Strategy	£445 375
October	IT strategy	Wales	IT	£184 864
June	Review	South	Strategy	£116 449
September	Implementation	Scotland	IT	£930 675

In addition to packages such as Compete!, there are also a number of more specialist applications for business forecasting. These could be used, for example, to handle the complicated competitive analysis part of a model, using a spreadsheet for the more straightforward analysis. One such product is called 4Thought for Windows, produced by Right International Systems Limited. 4Thought uses advanced mathematical theory to carry out an analysis similar to traditional regression analysis, but is claimed to provide a more realistic answer. It is over ten times more expensive than a spreadsheet.

Standard computer languages

It is also possible to use a standard computer programming language (such as COBOL, BASIC, Pascal or C) to program a financial model. Although this method provides the modeller with a completely clean slate, the effort involved in programming the initial model and any changes mean that very few organizations attempt this route.

To illustrate why, consider the operation of printing a page of a report. Whereas printing a page of a spreadsheet simply involves highlighting a range, the equivalent operation using a typical language involves specifying the layout of each item on the page, sending codes to tell the printer what fonts to use, when to make a form feed, a new page and so on. Taking this into account, it is difficult to conceive of a financial modelling application that could justify bespoke programming in place of a spreadsheet or modelling language.

Database packages

An alternative to a general programming language is to use the language provided with databases, such as Borland's Paradox and DBase IV. These databases give good file handling and printing facilities as well as a language more tailored to business uses. This makes programming substantially easier. Databases can be a useful solution if very large amounts of data need to be accessed and manipulated, or if the final model is to be used by non-experts. The reason for this is that many database languages tend to be much better at handling the screen and user input than the 'macro' languages provided with spreadsheets. They may also offer the ability to be compiled into machine language, which can then be run without the original application being present. This makes the distribution of planning and budgeting models to divisions, for example, much more cost-effective.

Ready-built models

Building financial models of any great size from scratch, be it on a spreadsheet or using some computer language, is always a time-consuming exercise. Recognizing this, several companies now market off-the-shelf business planning models. These request users to enter their data into existing logic. The model will almost certainly be automated in some way so as to guide users through this process and some help screens may also be provided should problems be encountered.

The models are often written as spreadsheets, with macros being used to automate the processes of inputting data, analysing and output. Some of the ready-made models available have been written using a programming language, which may offer benefits of speed and on-screen presentation over spreadsheet-based solutions. However, although both these types of model can be of use for quick analysis, typically they do not offer sufficient flexibility and power for more complicated applications, such as examining different capital structures, competitive assumptions and sophisticated cost allocation routines.

Notes

[1] The benchmarking of processor power all relate to Intel processors expressed using Intel's iCOMP™ rating index. Intel386, Intel486 and Pentium are Trademarks of Intel Corporation in the USA and other countries.

[2] Strictly speaking, versions of Windows versions X.X are not operating systems, but 'operating environments' as they themselves run as a program under DOS. The more sophisticated Windows NT, however, replaces DOS altogether.

7

PRINCIPLES OF MODEL BUILDING

INTRODUCTION

Model planning is the first step in producing robust models. The next stage is to ensure that the content of the plan is translated into a model that performs to specification. This can be achieved by adopting a few simple rules. The purpose of this chapter is to lay out the basis of such a system. The focus of the discussion will again be on spreadsheets, which is particularly relevant in this instance as spreadsheet-based models tend to have the greatest problems resulting from poor structuring.

A number of problems are commonly associated with spreadsheet models:

- large numbers of logic errors
- long model development times
- completed models are often difficult for non-expert users to run
- models are often difficult to read and follow
- models are difficult to update in the future.

The two solutions most commonly adopted for these problems are documentation and audit/testing. Most people would accept that it is only sensible to document a model, especially a large one, as this will help understanding at a later date. However, while documentation is often acknowledged as a good thing, modellers can be reluctant to develop and maintain suitable material. Documenting models is typically viewed as an afterthought, and an unchallenging one at that. Therefore, although it is still important to document models, it makes sense to build models in a way that will minimize the problems of poor, or missing, documentation.

The second solution, that of post-completion audit/testing, is also a useful discipline. Nevertheless, audits and testing are lengthy processes that can, at best, only be an incomplete check on the ability of the model to perform in all conditions. Both audits and documentation are examined further in Chapter 9. However, to say that a documented and audited model is an acceptable solution to ensuring model quality is too superficial a response to the major problems faced by spreadsheet models. The fundamental problems lie deeper; they are to do with the way in which models are built on spreadsheets. This chapter will lay out a set of principles to make spreadsheet models more reliable and understandable. It will then discuss how some of the features of modern spreadsheet packages can be used to make models both better presented and more manageable.

FOUR PRINCIPLES

Structuring a model properly involves no great mystery. There are four basic rules that, if followed, will make for accurate, efficient and readable models:

- build the model in modules
- separate data and logic completely
- be obvious, rather than clever, in designing formulae
- make the model self-documenting whereever possible.

Each of these points is discussed further below, and the Appendix to this chapter contains an example of a spreadsheet that reflects these principles.

Modularity

Modularity means that each discrete part of the model, such as costs or revenues, is designed so that *any alteration to the logic or data within any one module has no effect on any other module*. Ideally, this means that each module should be written as a 'black box', that is, it accepts input *from* a defined place and makes an output *to* a defined place, with whatever happens in between that is receiving an input and making an output being of no consequence to the rest of the model.

This practice, which is well-established in computer programming, will result in better models because:

- it reduces the scope for error by minimizing the number of interrelationships in the model
- it enables models to be more easily tested because the overall logic of the model can be tested before the bulk of the complex calculations have been input, then the detailed calculations can be tested in manageable units
- it allows changes to be made more safely, for example, if it is decided to change the method of calculating sales, there need be no worry that the balance sheet will suddenly stop to balance.

Financial models change frequently. It is difficult, therefore, to reconcile this need for flexibility with the rigour of defining the links between modules exactly in order that the black box principle can be applied in practice. For example, consider a typical revenue calculation. The data modules may contain information about the market size and its expected growth rate, as well as information about the firm's market share. All this information may be further subdivided by, say, product and sales area. If links were established between this data and the logic to calculate revenue, but it was wished to add a new product, then, using a conventional spreadsheet, the logic might still require a large-scale rewrite in order to accommodate the new product. Thus, although the black box principle is an ideal, it is not always completely achievable using spreadsheets.

The practical way in which we can move towards a black box model on a spreadsheet, is to keep the logical jumps in any one module small and to make frequent use of summaries. To illustrate this, consider the example of revenue calculation given above. There are various ways in which this problem could be laid out. One way is to use one formula to calculate the firm's revenue by multiplying together base market size, market growth rate, the firm's market share, its share growth rate and its price for each product within each sales area. Another approach is to use more modules, make smaller jumps at each one and produce a number of intermediate results, such as total market size, the firm's market share (in units) and *then* arrive at the firm's revenue. The steps involved in this second approach might look something like this.

Table 7.1

Module	Input form	Output to
Market data	Primary source	Market size and forecasts for growth
Firm's market share and price data	Primary source	Firm's market share and price modules
Market size	Market data	Revenue
Firm's market share (units)	Firm's market data	Revenue
Forecast price	Firm's market data	Revenue
Revenue	Market size, market share and price models	Cash flow, profit and loss account
Cash flow	Revenue	None
Profit and loss account	Revenue	None

Using this approach, the calculation of, say, market share is academic to the revenue module into which it feeds. The model can be constructed initially with no logic in the market share module, just a trial figure.

If all these steps had been condensed into one module, it would have resulted in a model with:

- complicated formulae, which are less easy to understand
- greater scope for error – partly because the formulae are more complicated, but also because the intermediate results, such as total market size (that is, the current market size multiplied by the growth rate), are unavailable to be checked for 'reasonableness'.

The multiple pages now offered by spreadsheets give the ideal opportunity to keep modules separate. In the case of smaller modules, which might not justify a separate page, it is still possible to keep them largely separate by placing one below another. The reason that they should not be put side by side is that columns typically represent time and, therefore, both are homogeneous and less likely to be deleted than rows. This means that the chance of changes to one module affecting other modules are less if a vertical alignment is used. If both columns *and* rows are likely to be changed and there are multiple modules on one sheet, then modules must be placed diagonally, running from the top left to bottom right of the spreadsheet (see Figure 7.1).

There are two further rules that should be considered when building modules:

- if at all possible, columns should be reserved to represent time, for example, column D as 1994 and so on, to make copying formulae easier and so reduce model development times
- on a similar theme, all the modules that feed into another module should have the same format as, again, this makes copying and formula building much easier.

Separation of data and logic

Modularity implies a basic separation of data and logic. Nevertheless, there is still often a temptation to add 'fudge factors' directly into lines of logic. For example, if staff costs are forecast to grow at 5 per cent per year, the formula would be: staff cost_t = staff $\text{cost}_{t-1} \times 1.05$. If, however, as is often the case, next year's figure is known with greater certainty, then it often seems easier to either adjust the 5 per cent growth rate for that year or to put in a figure in its place. Making either of these adjustments would be a quick fix,

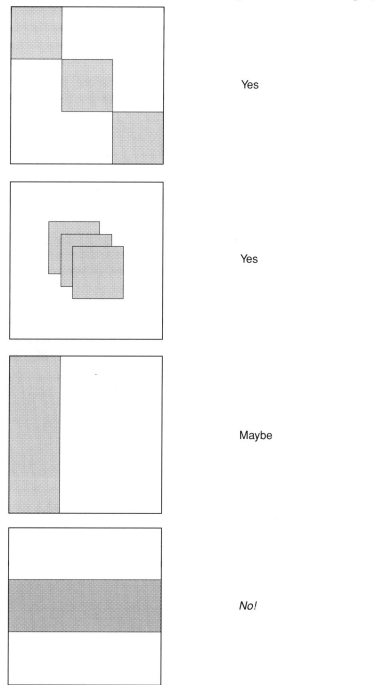

Yes

Yes

Maybe

No!

Figure 7.1 Layouts to use in spreadsheets to keep modules separate.

but it is also likely to be forgotten about by the person who has made the fix and might not be spotted by someone picking up the model for the first time. Spreadsheets make such fixes easy, but their use will fundamentally undermine the robustness of models.

The most important rule, which should be followed without exception, is that data and logic are not mixed in the same formula. The examples that follow illustrate what is, and is not, acceptable.

Table 7.2

Cell contents	Acceptable?	Reason
+A41	Yes	Formula only, no data
+A41+50	No	Mixes formula and data
@if(A41=A74, 'Yes', 'No')	Yes	Formula plus text acceptable
@if(A41=A74, 50, 40)	No	Mixes formula and data
@if(A41=A74, B3, B4)	Yes	Formula only
@if(A41=1, B3, B4)	Usually	Acceptable if the '1' will not change and its use if obvious
5,000	Yes	Data only
Fixed assets	Yes	Text only
+'Fixed assets ('&b5&')'	Yes	Text plus formula

If there is to be any hope of building robust models using spreadsheets, then these principles must be followed rigorously. Any deviation could easily be forgotten and result in decisions being made incorrectly as a result of the model. Following this style gives a certainty to a spreadsheet that is otherwise lacking. It also imposes a discipline that ensures *ad hoc* fixes are not made and forgotten about, but are clearly laid out.

The discussion so far has focused on keeping data and logic separate within individual cells. This split should be further emphasized by keeping data and logic in separate *modules*. The distinction should preferably also extend to designing models in which data can be saved separately from logic modules. This will enable different scenarios to be loaded into the model more easily, with the certainty that no unforeseen changes will be made to the logic.

Intuitive model design

The main aim of separating data and logic is to make it clear what to expect in a model. Intuitive models are models in which it is not only clear *what* to expect, but where that expectation *also* appears sensible and logical to most people. As with data-logic separation, there are two aspects to intuitive design:

- making formulae intuitive
- making the model layout and flow intuitive.

Making formulae intuitive is not always easy – there is often a temptation to get carried away and produce 'brilliant' formulae, such as:

@if(@if(B25=@max(B17,B45,B78),@vlookup(....))))))

These formulae may well be considerable feats of intellectual thought, but they are very difficult to understand. Intuitive formulae:

- are short
- do not use complicated functions unless absolutely essential or if they improve clarity
- are labelled clearly and/or specifically documented
- avoid nesting (such as, @if(@if(...)))
- avoid logical operators where possible (AND, NOT, OR) – particularly NOT
- use range names, not cell references, whenever practicable
- do not refer to cells that are in widely spaced physical locations.

An intuitive model layout has:

- formulae that are consistent across the whole length of a line, for example, if staff cost is +B42 for year 1, it would be expected to be +C42 for year 2, +D42 for year 3 and so on – it is all too common to see a model that goes year 1 +C42, year 2 +D101, year 3 +A5 – because, if a change is made to the line, the natural thing to do is to alter one year, then to copy its formula to subsequent years, but if the formulae are not consistent, then errors can clearly result;
- a logical flow from the top to the bottom of a sheet and from sheet/file A to B and so on;
- all columns referring to the same variable, preferably time
- levels of calculation made clear, for example:

sub-result 1
sub-result 2

RESULT A

Self-documentation

Models can be made more obvious through the use of descriptive text and comments. The motivation behind making a model self-documenting is two-fold. First, it is much easier to include a few notes as a model is built than it is to sit down afterwards and write screeds. Second, it is easier to follow a model that has documentation embedded in the sheet itself. Therefore, per-haps the safest rule is to assume that the model will not be fully documented once it is complete and so make labels self-documenting.

Self-documentation is neither difficult nor onerous – in common with all aspects of building a structured model – and soon becomes second nature. There are three main ways in which documentation can be added to models:

- a (standardized) descriptive section at the top of each module, listing the contents and purpose of the module and where inputs come from and go to and, if the module is complicated, a further box of free-form comments may be added
- making cell labels more descriptive, for example, in place of 'Staff cost' the label might read 'Staff cost – basic pay, incl. NIC & pensions'
- some spreadsheets offer the capability to attach notes to individual cells and these can be used for extra description.

APPENDIX: EXAMPLE OF STRUCTURED MODEL

Data module 1 of 2: market size data

Table 7.3

Contents	Historic market data by product and area for 1992; forecast for growth up to 1995	
Purpose	Data	
Inputs	From trade association forecasts	
Outputs	Logic module 1	

	1992 1000/units (Actual)	1993 % growth (Forecast)	1994 % growth (Forecast)	1995 % growth (Forecast)
Area 1				
Product 1	76.7	1.0%	1.0%	1.0%
Product 2	28.6	0.0%	−1.0%	−3.0%
Product 3	14.1	3.0%	2.5%	2.0%
Area 2				
Product 1	93.9	1.5%	1.5%	1.0%
Product 2	30.6	0.0%	−1.0%	−3.0%
Product 3	74.2	5.0%	5.0%	5.0%
Area 3				
Product 1	7.8	−3.0%	−3.0%	−5.0%
Product 2	78.2	1.0%	2.0%	4.0%
Product 3	11.1	−3.0%	−3.0%	−5.0%
Area 4				
Product 1	84.0	1.5%	1.5%	1.0%
Product 2	48.9	0.0%	1.0%	1.0%
Product 3	66.7	1.0%	1.5%	1.0%
Area 5				
Product 1	39.1	1.0%	1.0%	1.0%
Product 2	25.2	0.0%	0.0%	−1.0%
Product 3	99.6	1.0%	1.5%	1.5%
Total	778.7			

Data module 2 of 2: market share and price

Table 7.4

Contents	Historic and forecast data on our price and market share, by product and area
Purpose	Data
Inputs	From central marketing department
Output	Logic modules 2 and 3

Price analysis and forecast

	1992 (Actual)	1993 (Forecast)	1994 (Forecast)	1995 (Forecast)
Produce 1	$2.70	$2.81	£2.92	$3.04
Produce 2	$1.80	$1.87	$1.95	$2.02
Produce 3	$0.99	$1.03	$1.07	$1.11

Market share analysis

	1992 (Actual)	1993 (Forecast)	1994 (Forecast)	1995 (Forecast)
Area 1				
Product 1	5.4%	5.7%	6.1%	6.3%
Product 2	6.6%	7.5%	7.9%	8.2%
Product 3	7.7%	9.3%	10.1%	14.0%
Area 2				
Product 1	5.0%	3.0%	1.1%	0.0%
Product 2	3.2%	3.2%	3.3%	3.2%
Product 3	9.0%	10.8%	11.4%	12.5%
Area 3				
Product 1	7.1%	8.0%	8.3%	8.8%
Product 2	1.4%	0.0%	0.0%	0.0%
Product 3	0.2%	0.0%	0.0%	0.0%
Area 4				
Product 1	2.5%	2.2%	2.2%	2.0%
Product 2	1.3%	1.1%	1.0%	0.0%
Product 3	8.6%	8.3%	7.0%	6.6%
Area 5				
Product 1	0.6%	0.0%	0.0%	0.0%
Product 2	6.3%	7.3%	7.7%	8.0%
Product 3	9.1%	9.2%	8.9%	9.0%

Logic module 1 of 3: total market size

Table 7.5

Contents	Forecast of total market size			
Purpose	To provide input into the revenue calculation			
Inputs	Data module 1			
Output	Logic module 2			

1000 units	*1992* (Actual)	*1993* (Forecast)	*1994* (Forecast)	*1995* (Forecast)
Area 1				
Product 1	76.7	77.5	77.5	77.5
Product 2	28.6	28.6	28.3	27.7
Product 3	14.1	14.5	14.5	14.4
Area 2				
Product 1	93.9	95.3	95.3	94.8
Product 2	30.6	30.6	30.3	29.7
Product 3	74.2	77.9	77.9	77.9
Area 3				
Product 1	7.8	7.6	7.6	7.4
Product 2	78.2	79.0	79.8	81.3
Product 3	11.1	10.8	10.8	10.5
Area 4				
Product 1	84.0	85.3	85.3	84.8
Product 2	48.9	48.9	49.4	49.4
Product 3	66.7	67.4	67.7	67.4
Area 5				
Product 1	39.1	39.5	39.5	39.5
Product 2	25.2	25.2	25.2	24.9
Product 3	99.6	100.6	101.1	101.1
Total	778.7	788.5	790.0	788.4

Logic module 2 of 3: market share

Table 7.6

Contents	Forecast of our market share			
Purpose	To provide intput into the revenue calculation			
Inputs	Data module 1			
Output	Logic module 3			

1000 units	1992 (Actual)	1993 (Forecast)	1994 (Forecast)	1995 (Forecast)
Area 1				
Product 1	4.1	4.4	4.7	4.9
Product 2	1.9	2.1	2.2	2.3
Product 3	1.1	1.4	1.5	2.0
Area 2				
Product 1	4.7	2.9	1.0	0.0
Product 2	1.0	1.0	1.0	0.9
Product 3	6.7	8.4	8.9	9.7
Area 3				
Product 1	0.6	0.6	0.6	0.7
Product 2	1.1	0.0	0.0	0.0
Product 3	0.0	0.0	0.0	0.0
Area 4				
Product 1	2.1	1.9	1.9	1.7
Product 2	0.6	0.5	0.5	0.0
Product 3	5.7	5.6	4.7	4.4
Area 5				
Product 1	0.2	0.0	0.0	0.0
Product 2	1.6	1.8	1.9	2.0
Product 3	9.1	9.3	9.0	9.1
Total	40.5	39.9	38.0	37.7

Logic module 3 of 3: revenue

Table 7.7

Contents	Forecast of revenue
Purpose	To provide input into the financial statements
Inputs	Data module 2 and logic module 2
Outputs	Financial statements

£'000s	1992 (Actual)	1993 (Forecast)	1994 (Forecast)	1995 (Forecast)
Area 1				
Product 1	11.2	12.4	13.8	14.8
Product 2	3.4	4.0	4.4	4.6
Product 3	1.1	1.4	1.6	2.2
Area 2				
Product 1	12.7	8.0	3.1	0.0
Product 2	1.8	1.8	1.9	1.9
Product 3	6.6	8.7	9.5	10.8
Area 3				
Product 1	1.5	1.7	1.8	2.0
Product 2	2.0	0.0	0.0	0.0
Product 3	0.0	0.0	0.0	0.0
Area 4				
Product 1	5.7	5.3	5.5	5.2
Product 2	1.1	1.0	1.0	0.0
Product 3	5.7	5.8	5.1	5.0
Area 5				
Product 1	0.6	0.0	0.0	0.0
Product 2	2.9	3.4	3.8	4.0
Product 3	9.0	9.5	9.6	10.1
Total	65.2	63.0	61.0	60.7

8

TECHNIQUES FOR MODEL BUILDING

INTRODUCTION

By now, all the elements of designing, planning and preparing for the building of a model are in place. It is time to program the model on a computer. It is not the aim of this book to provide instruction in the software that should be used; that is the role of manuals and appropriate courses. However, there is a need to relate the capabilities of software, which may be very extensive, to the specific needs of financial modelling.

In a book of this size it would be impossible to provide guidance on model building covering all the possible software options discussed in Chapter 6. Indeed, the different features offered by software from competing manufacturers often vary so much as to make such general guidance rather academic anyway. As in other chapters, the focus here will be primarily on spreadsheet models. None the less, much of the following discussion may also be of relevance to models developed with alternative software.

Three main topics are examined, related to each of the three sections of a financial model, that is, data, logic and output. Under data, the linked issues of efficient data storage and manipulation are examined. Attention is then turned to making the most of the huge array of features that modern spreadsheets offer, first, for analysis and then presentation of models. Linkages to other software, particularly databases, are also examined where appropriate.

MODELLING DATA

It was noted in Chapter 4 that the data section of financial models is often neglected. This neglect extends not just to the amount of effort that is put into gathering and analysing data, but also to the way it is held within the model. Spreadsheets usually claim to have sophisticated data capabilities, but, in most cases, this is sadly far from the truth. This means that, even for models that use only fairly limited amounts of data, thought given to ways of best storing data is time well spent. The difference between a poorly and a well-designed data section can be significant in terms of the ease with which analysis can be carried out.

This section will examine how best to store data and will include an examination of whether data should be held on a spreadsheet at all. It is concluded that basic spreadsheets are inadequate for the data handling requirements of large models and that some form of database is required for such situations. The section concludes with a brief examination of the types of data manipulation that are applicable to financial modelling.

Data storage

Financial models often require quite substantial amounts of data to drive them. Some of this data will be historic and, therefore, unchanging, but other data may need to be altered quite regularly as different scenarios are run or the model is refined. It is also possible that, as the model is developed, the structure of the data will change. Therefore, data needs to be stored in a way that makes it easy to reorganize and change. It should also be stored efficiently, that is, so that access is fast and the space it takes up is minimized. Finally, the data should be organized so that it is reasonably independent from the model logic.

Software options

Spreadsheets are generally poor at meeting these requirements because they force data into one limited structure – rows, columns and sheets/files. Real data structures may be nothing like these – data will be related together in a variety of complicated ways. For example, sales data generated by an EPOS system in a chain of retail food shops might contain information about the products sold, which shop it was sold at, when it was sold and, perhaps, some transaction information, such as the number and value of items in the transaction in which the product was sold. Further databases may then be related to the sales database, giving information such as which region the shop is in, which department the product belongs to, and so on. The resultant chain of relationships would be difficult to show using a spreadsheet and would be inflexible once it were programmed.

The multidimensional analysis packages discussed in Chapter 6 clearly provide one means of dealing with this problem. Another method is to use a database. However, databases are poor at numerical analysis, such as NPV calculations, and so it may not be desirable to abandon the spreadsheet altogether. In this case, the objective should be to store the data on a database of some kind and to then relate that database to the spreadsheet. Data manipulation, such as reordering sales data from, say, a product to a customer view, can be done using the database, while complicated numerical manipulation can be left to the spreadsheet.

There are four main ways in which this concept can be implemented:

- download data from a database to a file that can be read by a spreadsheet
- use application-specific import and export features, such as import a DBase .dbf file into an Excel worksheet
- use the database features of the spreadsheet
- create a dynamic link (using DDE in Windows, for example) between database and spreadsheet.

The first method, using a file to affect the transfer, is the least desirable. There are several reasons for this:

- a manual operation is required to make the transfer, so it is easy for the link not to be updated
- the file that is created must be of a fixed format – both programs have got to know exactly where to put/get data – which is inflexible because the structure of the data cannot change
- it is likely that any special formatting information will be lost in the transfer, which means that there is an overhead to replace it manually after each exchange.

The second method, import and export features, suffers from broadly similar problems, only less so. For example, formatting information is more likely to be preserved in this method. Nevertheless it is still inflexible because it requires the same fixed format. The spreadsheet has to know in advance that last year's electricity cost, for example, will be imported to cell C34.

Although most spreadsheets offer poor database features, some are sufficiently advanced to make it feasible that data is held and manipulated using the spreadsheet's own data commands. Spreadsheets are constantly developing and so it is difficult to say that any one brand of spreadsheet is better than another for this. However, there are a number of key features to look for that will indicate if the database capability is sufficiently powerful:

- most spreadsheets require that the criteria for extract and query operations be entered into the spreadsheet itself – a rather cumbersome method – so spreadsheets that can handle these operations through other selection methods, such as menus and query boxes, are preferable, the spreadsheet should also provide for complicated logical queries, using combinations of 'and', 'or' and 'not' operators

- tools should be provided to produce revised data files, which show data from a different view, and these tools should be capable of multiple levels of analysis, such as producing sales by region, by branch, by product
- data entry and editing should be possible via a form, rather than as direct entry on to the spreadsheet.

Ideally, for a spreadsheet to be a real challenger to databases, it should also offer the ability to link different database files together using key fields. For example, one database might hold sales information and another details of products. If the two databases can be linked via, say, a common product code field, then information need only be stored once.

The final option is a dynamic link between spreadsheet and database. From the data manipulation point of view this solution is a clear winner as dedicated database packages, such as Borland's Paradox and Microsoft's Access, have powerful facilities to group, sort and analyse data, leaving the spreadsheet free to carry out numerical operations. The main drawback of the method is that it requires working with two different pieces of software. A multitasking operating system, such as Windows, makes this easier, but, none the less, the link needs to be established in a way that will preserve the independence between the data and logic sections. In this case, as with the option of using a data-capable spreadsheet, this means that links must be established based on named ranges or fields and not to specific cell references.

Data normalization

Although database systems may allow considerable flexibility in how data may be stored and accessed, when large volumes of data are involved, it is necessary to give thought to the most efficient means of storage. The efficiency of the model and, much more importantly, the robustness of the model to future changes, will be significantly affected by the decisions that are taken on the data storage structure of the database.[1] One means of determining how best to store data within the database is known as *normalization*. This is a technique used by systems analysts to reduce duplication and interdependencies in databases. In financial modelling terms, it ensures that the data section of the model is structured so that taking different 'views' of data is as easy as possible. Although normalization will not be needed for simple data, it is particularly useful for rationalizing data that has multiple layers (such as, country, region, district) and/or interdependencies (such as product name and product code number).

The stages of normalization will be illustrated here using the sales data from a chain of shops as an example. The shops are organized into a number of regions. Each shop sells a variety of products. Individual transaction information is held in the company's point-of-sale computer. A routine is run monthly to produce summarized information and it is this data that the model will use.

Normalization involves the following stages.

- Make a list of the data that is to be included in the model. In the example above these would be region name, region number, shop name, shop number, product name, product number, date (month for these purposes), amount of monthly sales for product. These 'attributes' describe the sales of the shop chain. Looked at from the point of view of the region the relationship can be written as (the italicized attributes are known as the 'primary key', which are the attributes that enable the record to be uniquely identified):

REGION (*Region Num*, Region Name, repeated group of shops {Shop Num, Shop Name, repeated group of product sales {Product Num, Product Name, Date, Amount}})

- The relationship above is organized by region and, within each region, there are a number of shops and each of these shops sell a number of products. The first step in normalization is to remove these 'repeating groups'. This is done by reorganising the relation based on the lowest level of attribute:

PRODUCT SALES (Region Num, Region Name, Shop Num, Shop Name, *Product Num*, Product Name, *Date*, Amount)
This relation is said to be in 'First Normal Form' (1NF).

- The second stage of transformation (from 1NF to second normal form (2NF)) is to separate out attributes that are not fully dependent on the primary key. For example, product name is only dependent on the product number and not on shop number or date. The 2NF is therefore:

SHOP SALES (*Product Num, Shop Num*, Region Num, Region Name, *Date*, Amount)
PRODUCT (*Product Num*, Product Name)
SHOP (*Shop Num*, Shop Name, Region Num).

- The third and, for our purposes, the final stage of normalization is to eliminate the dependencies between non-key attributes. The 3NF form is therefore:

SHOP SALES (*Product Num, Shop Num, Date*, Amount)
PRODUCT (*Product Num*, Product Name)
REGION (*Region Num*, Region Name)
SHOP (*Shop Num*, Shop Name, Region Num).

Data manipulation

The rationale for holding data in a database, not a spreadsheet, is that databases are better at manipulating data. This conclusion is often not accepted by the most hardened spreadsheet users – after all databases impose structure, while spreadsheets offer users unlimited flexibility in moving data into required formats. This position arises from a misunderstanding about the difference between, and roles of, data manipulation and what might be called numerical manipulation.

The difference between data and numerical manipulation can be made clearer if any piece of data, such as a series of operating costs, is thought of as having a series of attributes. In the case of operating cost, these might be the type of cost (defined by a cost, code and description), the money amount of cost, the period it refers to, cost driver and so on. Data manipulation is concerned with the analysis of any of these attributes; numercial analysis only with those that can be arithmetically, or mathematically, manipulated.

An example of data manipulation might be producing a list of operating costs sorted by cost code, another is extracting all the costs 'caused' by changes in production set-up. The most common operators in data manipulation are sorting, extracting and combining data to meet specified, logical conditions. Numerical manipulation varies from simple arithmetic operations, such as summing total operating cost, through to the more complicated, such as multiple regression analysis to forecast the cost stream into the future.

ANALYSIS TOOLS

The data manipulation tools just discussed will transform data into a format suitable for numerical analysis (referred to solely as 'analysis' from now on in this section). The role of analysis is varied, but includes:

- identifying trends
- making projections, possibly based on those trends
- allowing changes to variables by the user
- summarizing data
- transforming data, for example, depreciation calculation transforms the value of an asset over time
- calculating from base data, such as variable cost = 23% of sales.

This section will discuss some of the features offered by spreadsheets for these types of calculation under three headings: functions, commands and macros. It is not intended to be comprehensive, that is left to the manual, but, rather, a pointer to the kinds of tools that may be useful for financial modelling.

Functions

The majority of the analysis on a spreadsheet takes place using formulae entered into the sheet's grid of cells. A formula to add three cells would be +C24+C25+C26. Most users will also be familiar with the notion of using functions as part of formulae. These have special purposes, such as adding the contents of a range of cells. Thus, the formula above could be replaced with @sum(C24..C26)^2, which is easier to type and reduces the chance of the error of one cell being missed out.

Although some spreadsheet functions are widely known about, users are quite often unaware of the huge range of features now offered by the major packages. This section will take a look at functions, focusing in particular on:

- why functions can be useful
- types of function with applications
- pitfalls.

Why functions are useful

Spreadsheet manufacturers obviously place considerable importance on functions. In the case of one product, the function reference manual is over 500 pages long and describes literally hundreds of different functions. So, what benefits encourage such profligacy? As was noted previously, functions certainly save time. It is, for example much easier to use the @sum function than it is to pick each cell individually. They also reduce errors. Another benefit is that the resultant model will be more compact and probably easier to understand. There is also the added confidence that they have been tested and the algorithms they contain have been proved to work. Finally, functions are useful because they provide access to features of the spreadsheet that are not otherwise available. There is, for example, no command on Lotus 123 to calculate the standard deviation of a range; there is a function.

Types of function

Although there are many types of function, they all share the defining characteristic that they return a value. That value may be predetermined, for example, @NA, which makes a cell take the special value 'NA', or it may be determined as a result of input parameters. These parameters may be numbers, cell references or other functions. An example of a function with input parameters is @if(A24=1 'On','Off'), which will return 'On' if cell A24 = 1, or 'Off' otherwise.

A more useful classification of function is by category. Common categories of function include:

- financial
- logical
- text
- statistical
- mathematical
- other functions, including date/time, spreadsheet status/information, database.

Functions in each of these categories are potentially of use to the financial modeller. The discussion here, though, will be limited to giving a flavour of each type.

Financial functions

Many financial models make some use of the financial functions built into spreadsheets, such as @NPV and @IRR. There are a number of others, too, that can be helpful, but are less commonly used. These include functions for depreciation, annuities and compound interest.

The main thing to be aware of when using these functions is to be clear about the formulas on which they are based and NPV is a case in point. The @NPV function in Lotus, for example, discounts the first cash flow. The formula in Chapter 2 assumes that the first cash flow happens immediately and so it is not discounted. The @NPV function, therefore, offers less flexibility in calculation than manually dividing each cash flow by $(1+i)^t$ and summing them. The @IRR function, therefore, returns the discount rate at which the @NPV is zero.

Logical functions

Logical functions allow choices to be made in models. Some logical functions will make a cell display a different result depending on a predefined condition being met. Others provide tests of logical conditions.

There are two main functions that allow cells to take a different value depending on various conditions: @if and @choose. The function @if makes a choice between one of two possible outcomes and @choose between one of many. The former is the more commonly used of the two. There are a great number of possible uses of these functions. One of the most common uses of The format is to 'switch' between different sets of assumptions. For example, if sales growth can be expressed either in terms of sales area or product group growth rates, then @if can choose the suitable rate to use. To do this, a cell is set up that has a 0 in it if sales growth rate is to be used and a 1 if product growth rate is used.

Another useful application of @if is in error checking. Although a properly designed model will minimize the risk of embarrassing errors, such as the balance sheet not balancing, they can never be eliminated altogether. All too often, these errors happen when many changes have been made and everyone is tired. Printouts may not always be checked as carefully as normally. Therefore, it is sensible to at least be warned that something has gone wrong. The @if function can be used for this. For example, to check if the balance sheet balances, a row can be set up where each cell is of the form @if(C132=C137,0,1), where C132 and C137 are the two sides of the balance sheet. Then, in a separate part of the model, another cell can sum all the years and if the sum is greater than 0 it can report an error, for example, @if(@sum(C140..H140)=0,'OK','ERROR'). A whole set of these could be set up to produce a status report on the model. The print macro can even check them to give a warning before printing if there are any errors.

A number of functions are provided for use with @if and @choose. These allow certain conditions to be checked, such as whether a condition is true (@true), false (@false) or if the cell would return an ERR (@iserr), such as dividing by zero.

Text functions

Text in computer jargon is known as *strings*. The spreadsheet will interpret the contents of a cell as a string if the first character of the entry is a character and not a number or function definer (such as @ in Lotus 123). There are lots of operations that can be performed on strings, such as:

- subdivide them into smaller strings
- add pieces of separate strings together to make new strings
- set up models in which *all* headings change when just *one* does.

There are a wide variety of commands that can be used to manipulate strings. Some of the principal ones are as follows.

Table 8.1

Name	Function	Example
@left	Takes the first x characters in a string	@left('Frederick',4) = 'Fred'
@right	Takes the last x characters in a string	@right{'Omnibus',3) = 'bus'
@mid	Extracts the middle x characters from a string, starting y characters in from the left	@mid('Frederick Bloggs Esquire',11,6) = 'Bloggs'
@trim	Removes any spaces before, or after, a string	@trim(' Model ') = 'Model'

The need to subdivide strings is not going to arise all that often in financial modelling. The main uses are likely to be in abbreviating headings. For example, if the data module contains a list of detailed headings for different types of cost, these functions may be used to reproduce the headings in a shorter form in another part of the spreadsheet. It is a good practice to link headings together in the same way as numbers. Therefore, if one row has formula +C30, D30 and so, then the row description should relate back to the row heading in line 30, for example, +A30.

Other useful string functions include @upper, which will convert a string into upper case, and @lower, which does the opposite. The function @proper will convert 'fred blOGgS' into 'Fred Bloggs', while @find can locate one string within another. The @find function can be used in conjunction with @mid to decide the starting point to extract a substring. The function @replace could then substitute another string for the extracted one, such as:

@mid('Frederick Bloggs Esquire',@find('Es'),3) = 'Esq'

Strings can be added together in a similar fashion to numbers, so that for example, +'Fred'&'erick' gives 'Frederick'. This starts to become useful when the contents of cells are used as well as actual text. Numbers can also be incorporated into the string by converting them into strings using the @string command. For example, if various levels of unit cost were being modelled, it might be useful for these to be shown at the top of each page. Therefore a label could be placed in the top border. For example:

+'*** Unit Cost of £'&@string(C388,2)&' Used ***'

that, if unit costs were £2.73, would give:

*** Unit Cost of £2.73 Used ***

Statistical and mathematical functions

The range of statistical functions provided by spreadsheets varies quite widely. The vast majority of packages provide functions to calculate simple statistics such as average, standard deviation, maximum and minimum. The most advanced can return a variety of statistical distributions, such as normal, Poisson, lognormal, binomial, Chi and so on. These functions can be used to carry out quite sophisticated data analysis on data such as customer survey results and queuing statistics. The facility also offers the prospect of developing advanced financial models that use Monte Carlo simulation in place of the normal sensitivity approach (this is discussed further later in this chapter under Commands).

As well as these statistical functions, spreadsheets have a range of mathematical functions, such as trigonometric functions and logarithms. For the most part, these are not likely to be particularly heavily used in financial modelling, but they may still find a use. For example, a part of a sine curve, like the one shown in Figure 8.1 (created by @sin), can be a useful approximation of the S-shaped curve that sales are postulated to follow in response to increased advertising expenditure.

Another potentially useful set of mathematical functions are matrix functions. In mathematical terms, a matrix is a table of numbers arranged in rows and columns, just like a spreadsheet. There are a number of operations that can be performed on a matrix, such as addition and multiplication, and some packages offer matrix arithmetic as a function. While the more imaginative modellers can no doubt find many esoteric uses for these capabilities, matrix multiplication functions provide a way of easily producing, say, a total stock

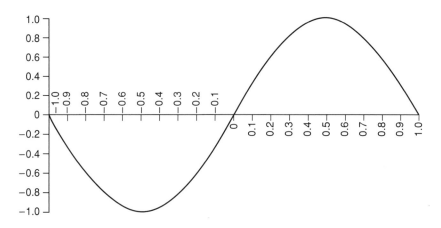

Figure 8.1 A sine curve created using a spreadsheet function.

value from a database of stock quantities and costs. Instead of calculating stock × cost for each stock line, one simple matrix product can be calculated that multiplies the stock matrix by the cost matrix.

Commands

Commands are used to build and maintain the spreadsheet model. They are accessed using a mouse or keyboard from menus of text and icons on the screen. Most commands, such as move, copy, print and so on are very familiar to anyone with more than a passing knowledge of spreadsheets. The more recent versions of packages have expanded the range of commands away from the purely housekeeping ones further into the analysis arena.

The built-in range of commands can be further extended in some packages by the use of spreadsheet 'add-on' programs. These may be supplied either by the package manufacturer or by some third party. In some cases, these add-ons eventually become part of the basic package.

Commands designed to assist with analysis include goal seeking, complicated statistical analysis, multiple regression, moving averages, worksheet consolidation, Monte Carlo analysis and sensitivity analysis. The range, particularly from third-party add-on providers, is constantly growing. There are too many commands to discuss in detail here so the focus will therefore be on two key, but less well known, analysis commands: goal seeking, which is now built in to all three major packages, and Monte Carlo simulation, which is available as an add-in program for Lotus 123 and Excel.

Goal seeking

Goal seeking is a command that enables a spreadsheet to alter the values of specified variables automatically in order to maximize, minimize or target some objective, possibly subject to constraints. This is a very powerful tool that, although available as a third-party add-on for some time, is only recently being bundled into spreadsheet packages. Goal seeking is one of the features of the new generation of spreadsheets that can make the most difference to the power of spreadsheet-based models.

Generally, there are two types of goal seeking provided with spreadsheets. The first, simpler, type allows the user to set a target for a variable, such as profit, and then specify a variable to alter in order to reach the desired target. This can have a number of uses. It could be used to work out the price that would have to be charged to give a profit of £x or it could determine by how much unit variable costs would have to be reduced in order to reach the same profit. While these questions might be quite simple to solve on a straightforward spreadsheet that perhaps just assumed that price changes did not affect sales, on a more sophisticated model with competition assumptions built in, the goal seeking can save substantial effort.

The second type of goal seeking removes the need to specify a target level for the objective. Instead, the command can be instructed to maximize or minimize. The ability to add constraints is also available. This facility can be used to solve problems such as:

- setting the gearing level so as to maximize the return on equity, subject to maintaining a specified debt service coverage ratio
- maximizing market share in x years hence, subject to maintaining specified profit levels
- developing a manpower plan to minimize staff costs, but to meet forecast demand levels
- setting the profit maximizing price, subject to competitive and customer reactions
- structuring a joint venture agreement to maximize the profit of the major partner, subject to prespecified returns accruing to the minor partner.

The possibilities are more or less limited solely by the structure of the model. In the simplest models, goal seeking will be of little benefit – it may alleviate the need for a few sums, but little more. In complicated models, it can provide a whole new dimension to modelling. Nevertheless, all that goal seeking can do is to work within the framework of the logic and data already specified in the model; it cannot make up for unrealistic assumptions. In fact, it will compound the effect of a poorly researched model by adding an extra layer of credibility to the results – nothing seems more definitive than an output along the lines of 'a price of £2.43 maximizes profit'. As usual the 'rubbish in, rubbish out' maxim applies.

Monte Carlo simulation

Monte Carlo simulation is the name given to a model that uses probability distributions instead of fixed numbers to describe certain variables. For example, in a normal model, a sales forecast might be input as £120 000, but in a Monte Carlo model it might be input as 'normally distributed around a mean of £120 000 with a standard deviation of £25 000'. The model would then be run many times and a frequency distribution produced showing the results. This method allows the *most likely* result to be obtained.

Macros

The final group of tools that spreadsheets offer the financial modeller are macros. At its most basic level this is a facility to automate a series of key-strokes. Therefore, a macro might be set up to format a cell in a particular way and then, instead of having to enter a number of commands each time that operation was performed, it would simply be necessary to run the macro. At a more sophisticated level, macros offer a rudimentary programming language that can be used to automate the operation of a model entirely and so de-skill the running of sensitivity analysis and the like.

Macro commands can also be used to perform operations that would be difficult, or even impossible, to incorporate into the spreadsheet logic. For example, spreadsheet database handling facilities have tended to be poor and macros offer a way of getting round this problem. If, say, data is input into one sheet and it needs to be sorted into categories, then presented in a different format in another sheet, macros provide the ability to automate the series of operations necessary to do this in a way that simple formulae could not.

There are six types of command offered by macros:

- normal commands, such as formatting, printing, adding rows and so on
- programme control commands that allow the macro to make basic decisions and control the flow of the macro
- movement commands that will move the cursor around, replicating the function of the cursor keys or mouse
- data input commands that stop the operation of the macro to accept input from files or from the user
- screen control commands that improve presentation when running a macro
- file control commands that make data handling easier.

A lot can be achieved by macros. There have been examples of quite large firms actually programming their accounting and time-recording systems using them. However, with the best will in the world, macros are not up to complicated programming tasks. They do not offer the flexibility and, above all, the structure that is required. They are also slow and difficult to debug, although most spreadsheets offer some form of simple macro-debugging tools. Of all the component parts of spreadsheets, macros appear to have developed least over the years. However, perhaps this is understandable, because, as spreadsheets develop further in the facilities and ease of use that they offer, the use of macros as 'fixes' for inadequacies of the spreadsheets themselves can be expected to decline.

PRESENTATION

There are at least two good reasons to care about the presentation of financial models. The first is because financial models are selling documents. Most people do not wake up one morning and think 'I am a bit bored today, I think I will build a financial model'. They might wake up and think 'I am seeing the bank next week, I had better put together some financial forecasts pretty fast if I want that new loan'. However much effort is put into elegant algorithms and sophisticated data structures, it will be wasted if the message of the model is not plainly clear to a reader.

Presentation is also important to financial models because they are inherently complicated and involved. If they are not clearly presented, there is little hope of someone who has not been intimately involved in their construction being able to know what is going on.

Presentation, then, is all about improving clarity; about getting messages across more clearly. It would, of course, be naive to suggest that it is always desirable for every aspect of a model to be clearly conveyed. The division requiring funds for a new project will want selectively to emphasize the most palatable parts of its project to head office. It could do this by fiddling the figures or, if it were slightly more sensible, it could do it through presentation.

Good presentation is a combination of adhering to the principles of model design discussed in the last chapter and using the features available in software. Spreadsheets are now some of the best presentation tools on the market. Some of their capabilities are as follows.

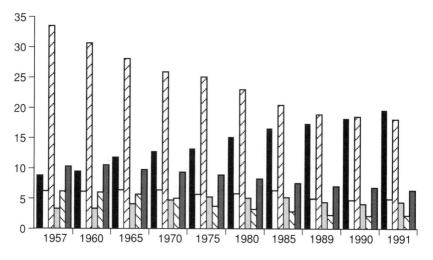

Figure 8.2 Old-fashioned presentation of a graph.

Graphs

Spreadsheets have always been able to draw graphs, but they used to look like the one in Figure 8.2 and had to be printed separately from the spreadsheet. They now look like the one Figure 8.3 and can be incorporated into any position within a spreadsheet.

Carefully selected and placed, graphs can add considerable weight to a spreadsheet. For example instead of a plain old table of key performance indicators, graphs could be used to show forecast improvements.

Enhancements to the text

Graphs are useful, but the core of a financial model will always be tables of numbers. However, these can be confusing, cramped and difficult to read, or they can be clear. To make them clear, spreadsheets offer a variety of tools.

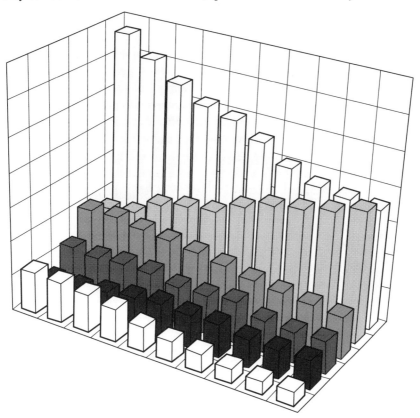

Figure 8.3 A graph produced by an up-to-date spreadsheet.

The first tool – number formatting – has been around a long time, but is still often ignored. Too many spreadsheets still have numbers that read 52347883.2654, whereas they could read 52,347,883. The use of the comma format is vital for large numbers, as is the suppression of spuriously accurate decimal places. In fact, in most cases even showing the above number with commas is insufficient – the spreadsheet might be better given just in £'000s and the number shown as 52,348. It is important to note that the method being talked about here only *displays* numbers differently, it does not alter how they are stored within the spreadsheet.

Newer versions of spreadsheets take text enhancement a lot further than number formatting by providing facilities to draw lines, shade cells, add symbols and use different sizes and styles of text (fonts). Using these capabilities, models can be made clearer and easier to understand.

Other features

Some spreadsheets offer further presentation features. For example, Microsoft Excel 4 and later versions have an outlining feature that can be used to show variable levels of detail in a model. A profit and loss account might be made up of lines for each of a number of subsidiaries. Outlining could be used to show all the detail, a consolidation to, say, regional level or only the highest level detail, as required. Other spreadsheets have sophisticated drawing and slide show facilities. Borland's Quattro Pro is one of the most advanced in this area. It is, for example, capable of displaying slides one after another, with each slide 'melting' into the next one. Having this facility on the same piece of software used to develop the model can significantly reduce the time needed to make presentations.

Notes

[1] The term 'database' is used to refer to an area/file separate from the model logic. It could be a spreadsheet file or a file of a database package such as DBase IV.

[2] The convention that is used to identify a function varies between spreadsheets. For example, Excel begins formulae with '=', whereas Lotus 123 and others use '@'. For the sake of simplicity the @ convention will be adopted here.

9

QUALITY CONTROL

INTRODUCTION

Financial models are often critical in decisions such as deciding whether or not to make an investment, selecting a strategy to pursue or determining the price to charge for a service. Research[1] suggests, however, that the vast majority of financial models in existence have one or more significant errors. One of the main messages of this book has been that quality control, in the form of a structured approach to modelling, should be applied throughout the planning, design and building of models. Many of these errors occur because models are not built in a sufficiently rigorous way and a poorly built model is unlikely ever to be free of errors. Nevertheless, even if models are built in a structured fashion, there is still always the potential for error. Some form of quality control process, therefore, is also necessary after model building has been completed and when the model is being used.

Model errors are of three types: errors in data, errors in the logic when the model is first created and errors that creep into the logic during the running of the model. Identifying existing errors requires that the model be thoroughly tested prior to use, while ensuring that further errors do not occur demands some procedures for running the model and making changes to the logic in a controllable fashion.

Validity of data and assumptions

Financial models often have quite a large volume of data and assumptions driving them and these clearly must be correct for the model to be valid. On one level, therefore, there is a need to check that data has been correctly inputted. This is simply a matter of printing off the data modules and carefully comparing them with the source documents. Because all data will be in one place and will not be mixed into formulae, this will be straightforward, if rather tedious. None the less it is surprising how often this simple check is not carried out. If large volumes of data have been inputted, it is quite likely that there will be at least some inputting errors.

On a different level, the assumptions made in the model must be defensible and realistic. Deciding on exactly what is realistic cannot simply be a matter of checking a printout. How this check is done will be up to individual preference, but, in the case of a large model, it is often worth gathering together key individuals for a few hours to review the assumptions used. A workshop format, where one person acts as 'facilitator' to guide discussion, may be useful. As well as providing a format for a range of key people to see the assumptions as a totality, a workshop also offers the chance to communicate the state of the model widely and to seek wide support for its assumptions.

A final point to consider in validating data is whether formulae are logically correct. For example take the formula 'variable cost = 76% of fixed cost'. Typically, this would have been arrived at by looking at the current relationship between fixed and variable costs. However, this relationship does not imply that variable cost is related to fixed cost in a certain way, only that it happens to be a certain portion at a given point in time. So the relationship may not hold once fixed costs change. If this is the case, then the formula is logically incorrect. Logically inaccuracies cannot be detected from examination of formulae, thus making a workshop approach particularly useful.

ERROR CHECKING

Introduction

As well as ensuring the validity of data, the logic built into the model must be thoroughly tested to ensure that it behaves as expected, both with existing and other (possibly more extreme) data. This level of testing is important to ascertain that the model is producing the correct result not only now, but will also continue to do so if alternative scenarios, or revised data, are run.

Testing is often not carried out because, aside from laziness, there is a tendency to believe that errors will be obvious once real data is used. This may not be the case, particularly in a complicated model, as after all, if the result is obvious then what is the point of having a model at all? Testing can also help identify the bounds of the model, that is the ranges of input within which the logic accurately reflects reality.

In some ways, building a financial model is akin to writing a computer program. A computer program will always be (or at least should always be) tested to ensure that it meets its specification. Although many of the processes involved in building a financial model are derived from mainstream computer programming, most financial models do not have a written specification in the same amount of detail as an equivalent-sized program. Testing models, therefore, often involves elements of art as well as science – results should generally look right in business terms as well as being logically correct in modelling terms.

Although reasonableness is a useful test, it can only be a part of the answer. In some cases results may be generated by the model that are not necessarily intuitive, but that is not to say they are wrong. After all, there would be little point in financial modelling if it only ever produced results that could be predicted without the model ever having been built. The underlying logic of models must be tested to ensure that it works as intended.

There are two main ways of testing the logic, namely manual checking of calculations using test data and tracing of logic paths with software audit tools. It is likely that both these tools would be used in combination.

Use of test data

Models are often built around the data that is available. This can result in models that produce an expected result, almost by definition. In the course of running a model developed in this way, it is quite common to discover some significant error that only showed up when the input data changed from the original data. Even models that have not been designed like this will sometimes fail if data changes dramatically. Setting values to zero, in particular, often results in problems by generating untrapped divide by zero errors.

Running the model using test data designed to flag these difficulties means that errors can be spotted early on and ironed out before the model is used. Therefore, the design of test data is important in order to show up as many problems as possible.

In theory, the objective of model testing should be to test all the logic paths, or choices, in the model. In practice, a financial model may have a vast number of possible routes, many of which will be interrelated. It is, therefore, often not easy to identify all the potential paths and it would not be practical to test them all. The following points can be considered in deciding how extensively to test:

- a model does not have to cope with any conceivable situation, for example, if setting revenue equal to zero produces an error, it is really unlikely to matter as the proposition being modelled has completely failed anyway, but what might be more important is if the gearing level is changed to eliminate debt and zero debt produces an error

- it is important to remember that the objective is to *really* test the model – in fact, to try and make it fail (there is often the temptation for modellers who have worked long and hard to build a model to almost subconsciously test the model so that it does *not* fail, but testing must be ruthless)
- it follows that the people responsible for building the model may not be the best choice when it comes to spotting errors thrown up by test data. As well as an understandable pride in their creation, they may be too involved in the detail to step back and see the overall picture or they may simply not have enough knowledge of the business being modelled to judge if something is wrong
- all switches in the model should be tried at both off and on, for example, if there is a switch to either pay, or not pay, dividends both settings need to be tried out
- assumptions that act as a sort of variable switch, such as the debt/equity ratio, should be tested across a wide range of values, preferably including extreme values, such as 0 per cent and 100 per cent in this case
- it is often useful to enter large numbers to check that column widths are adequate on reports
- as well as checking the results of a test run visually for obvious errors, it is also important to calculate the expected result manually in a number of cases.

Use of software audit tools

Running test data through a model will often show up that something is wrong. It may then be quite difficult to find out exactly what the problem is. It is to be hoped that, if the test data has been carefully constructed and the test programme run in a structured fashion, changing variables one at a time and calculating the effects of each change, then locating the error should be comparatively straightforward. Life is rarely like that, though, and this is where software audit tools may help.

Most of the current versions of the major spreadsheet packages offer some form of audit commands. These vary in their usefulness, but typically offer the ability to trace dependencies and relationships from one formula throughout the model. Therefore if, say, the gearing level was altered and this caused the balance sheet to stop balancing, the audit program could be run to highlight each cell that referred to the gearing ratio. Whether or not this is actually a function that will help resolve the problem is a moot point, though, because of the potential complexity of the relationships involved.

Other functions offered by audit programs include turning the display into a 'map' that shows formulae as, say, an 'F', numbers as an 'N' and so on.

This is useful for quickly identifying any fixes that have been hidden away in a line that should be all formulae. Audit tools will also typically identify the relationships that have resulted in a CIRCular reference. This can provide a useful first pass for identifying and eliminating any unwanted CIRCs.

In general, software audit tools can be useful if all else fails, but their use in practice is often rather limited as they do little to overcome the basic problem of financial models, which is their inherent complexity.

KEEPING MODELS ERROR-FREE

Testing a model should ensure that the vast majority of problems left after model building are located and eliminated. It will also help establish the bounds within which the model can be operated. What it will not do is stop errors creeping back into the model once it is being used. These sorts of errors are the, more or less inevitable, result of running a complicated model under severe time pressure. Complicated models and short deadlines are found in the most critical applications, such as evaluating acquisition targets, assessing corporate planning options and project appraisal. By implication, it is the most important applications that are likely to face the severest problems in keeping errors from entering the model.

So, why should it be inevitable that errors will creep into models? The basic cause is that model logic is rarely set in stone, it will develop during the life of the model to reflect new understandings gained. For example, while modelling a given product's market, research may reveal that the main determinant of market share is the leading competitor's price, not advertising spend as was previously thought. The calculation of market share and, hence, revenue therefore needs to be adjusted, that is, the logic is changed.

Every time that the logic is changed, errors may occur. These are of two main types. First, errors from mistyping a formula and second, errors from using different versions of logic with different runs or scenarios of the model.

Mistyping formulae

Simply mistyping a formula is easily done. An example might be to use +A42 × H32, instead of +A42 × H31. In this case, range names could have been used to minimize the chance of error and the formula might have been +PRICE × QUANTITY. The ease with which errors can be made means that it is important quickly to retest parts of the model when changes have been made. Building a model in a modular fashion enables this to be done more easily.

Versions and scenarios

The most serious problems that result from the model logic being changed during the life of a model come from mismatches between a particular version of the logic and different runs. Take, for example, a model built to evaluate the financing impact of different company structures. If there are four structures being looked at, then four runs (or *scenarios*) of the model will be required. Changing a part of the logic (that is, changing the *version* of the model) means that each scenario must be rerun with the new logic.

If data and logic are entirely separate and independent, then this can be accomplished relatively simply. However, this is rarely the case and one of two things normally happens:

- the logic is manually changed in each scenario separately, so there is a possibility of an error occuring with each change
- older scenarios, which are maybe no longer used, are not changed, which means that it is difficult to know which version of logic is used by which scenario and, if an old scenario is reused, it may have an incorrect version of logic with it.

The only effective way of overcoming this problem is to ensure that data and logic are independent. Each scenario can then be rerun with any new version of logic. This must be backed up by documentation of each version and scenario.

DOCUMENTING MODELS

There seems to be an unwritten rule of financial modelling, that, even if a model works now, it may not work indefinitely. One of the major reasons is that, when data changes, the model takes some as yet unused logic branch, which produces an error. The testing routines discussed above are designed to help trap this. However, even if models are thoroughly tested and proved to work with all conceivable data now, events can still happen to cause errors in the future.

The most common event of this sort is a change to the logic that results in a number of unexpected side-effects. The most common reasons for this are:

- the model is badly laid out and/or not properly structured and, as a result, a change has a number of unintentional side-effects
- the logic is so complicated that its rationale is quickly forgotten
- the model is large and, however well laid out, will inevitably be quite complicated because the system it is modelling is complicated.

In the first two cases, the solution is to build models according to the princi-ples outlined in the last chapter. The last problem, though, will always exist. The only sensible solution is to document the model adequately.

Documenting models is something that modellers seem to hate – it is seen as boring, time-consuming and essentially uncreative, all very unlike build-ing the model itself. There are no miraculous solutions to this, except to remember that it is usually not *that* bad, saves a tremendous amount of pain later and produces an altogether more professional end result.

The documentation for a model will have at least three sections

- *Data Sources*, relevant dates, people responsible for collection.
- *Logic* What each module does and how it works, with a particular focus on explaining the more complicated routines in a manner that can be understood by someone who has never come across the model before.
- *Version/scenario information* Each development of a model should be given a version number (one each for logic and for data) that should be displayed on each printout. A useful convention is that all 'development' versions of the model are labelled version 0.xy, with x increasing to rep-resent major changes, and y minor ones: all operational versions are labelled x.y, with the same convention, but where x>=1. The basic docu-mentation should refer to a given version number, with changes between that version and the last clearly listed and annotated to show the reason for the change – particularly if the change was due to an error. Scenarios should be given similar, but separate, code numbers. Thus, one run of a model might be:

Version 1.20

Scenario 3.4

Some models may have a further section of operating instructions, which provide a guide to its use for non-expert users. This may be useful if macros have been used to allow, say, data to be inputted by clerical staff.

Note

[1] For example, a study by accountants Coopers and Lybrand, quoted in the *Strategic Planning Society News* (October 1992), found that 'nine out of ten spreadsheet models contain at least one significant mistake'.

Part IV

MODEL BUILDING AND INTERPRETATION IN PRACTICE

10

BUILDING A FULL-SIZED MODEL

INTRODUCTION

This book has sought to give a practical approach to the planning, design and construction of accurate financial models that will help business decision making. A number of comparatively simple examples have been used to illustrate particular aspects of the modelling process. However, in many real situations, models need to be quite large and complicated to represent adequately the business, or project, being examined. The purpose of this chapter therefore, is, to work through the logic of a full-sized example to show how a structured approach is used on a real project.

The example used is a project appraisal in manufacturing industry. It is fictional, although very loosely based on a real example. For simplicity, tax is ignored. The example will concentrate on the model's construction as model interpretation is examined in Chapter 11.

THE PROBLEM

Background

A large waste management company (Ecowaste of Sweden) is considering expansion of its existing UK waste paper collection business by building its own plant to recycle waste newspapers into new newsprint. The company currently sells the waste it collects to a third party who use the paper in their mill.

Ecowaste see a number of potential attractions to the project, such as improved security of offtake for their waste collection operation, potentially quite high financial returns and diversification into a new area. Nevertheless, the Board wishes to assure itself that the project is economically viable and wants to know whether it could be financed making use of limited recourse project financing. Therefore, it has been decided to build a financial model.

Existing operation

Ecowaste collected 96 300 tonnes of waste newspaper in 1993 in the UK. This was sold to a mill for recycling at an average price of £49 per tonne.

Collection is made from three sources:

- directly from newspaper publishers (45 000 tonnes)
- via local councils' recycling schemes (25 700 tonnes)
- from direct collection contracts with large companies (25 600 tonnes).

In each case, Ecowaste use their own road transport to transport the waste to a central storage depot, where it is stored prior to periodic rail collection by the mill.

Ecowaste pay the following rates:

- Newspaper publishers, £33.42 per tonne
- Local councils, £28.50 per tonne
- Direct collection, £27.70 per tonne.

Ecowaste has a fleet of 7 lorries, which cost £70 000 each when new 3 years ago. They are expected to have a life of five years, over which they are depreciated using the reducing balance method. They are expected to be sold for £25 000 at the end of their life. The running costs of each lorry are £25 000 per year. When the lorries reach the end of their life, it is not planned to buy replacements, instead making use of leasing.

The central warehouse facility has the following annual costs:

- heat & light, £10 111
- staff, £32 470
- business rates, £7 200
- machinery maintenance, £1 890
- building maintenance, £2 009
- consumables, £4 984

Depreciation on the building is £25 000 per annum.

The proposed mill

Basic economics

The proposed mill site is adjacent to the existing warehouse facility. The planned mill configuration is designed to produce 100 000 tonnes of recycled paper each year. The bulk of the input will be waste newsprint, but some pulp will also be required to keep the quality of the final paper sufficiently high. The plant will require 117 400 tonnes of waste paper and 22 119 tonnes of bought in pulp per annum.

Ecowaste plan to expand their waste collection operation to provide the additional waste. Contracts have so far been agreed for an additional 15 000 tonnes from a newspaper publisher, at the slightly higher price of £35 per tonne. It is hoped to collect the remaining 6 100 tonnes from local councils at the existing rate of £28.50. Preliminary investigation suggests that pulp will cost £300 per tonne delivered.

The technical advisors to the project (The PaperCons Partnership) forecast that the recycled paper can be sold for £375 per tonne less delivery costs (by a third party) of £20 per tonne.

Variable operating costs

Apart from the cost of buying in paper and pulp, the other major variable operating costs are chemicals, to remove the ink from the incoming waste paper, and power for machinery. These are as follows.

Table 10.1

Cost type	Cost per tonne of newsprint produced
Fuel oil for boiler	£12.03
Electricity	£24.19
De-inking chemicals	£38.41
Maintenance	£7.50
Other consumables	£24.33

It can be assumed that the relationship between variable costs and production output is linear from an output of 40 000 tonnes per annum up to the plant capacity of 100 000 tonnes per annum. However, if annual output is below 60 000 tonnes, it can be assumed that unit variable costs will be 12 per cent higher. The relationship is no longer accurate below a production of 40 000 tonnes per annum.

Fixed operating costs

The fixed costs are taken to be those that will be held constant over short-term changes in the plant output. Longer term fluctuations in demand, or the adoption of new processes in the future, may affect these costs. The main fixed cost is staff.

Table 10.2

Staff	Number	Average cost per person
Production	80	£12 000
Supervisors	7	£15 750
Maintenance	12	£13 000
Sales	3	£10 000 + 0.25% of sales value over 80 000 tonnes/year
Management	3	£25 000
Administration	6	£13 800

Other fixed costs are as follows:

Table 10.3

Cost	Annual amount
Lease of forklift trucks and lorries	£1.38m
Business rates	£0.50m
Office costs – telephone, fax, etc.	£0.04m

The cost of heat, light and miscellaneous power in included in the variable cost electricity figure.

Capital costs

The construction period is planned to be 24 months, starting immediately after the land purchase is completed. The land purchase is expected to be completed by the end of December 1994. The mill can begin full operation immediately after completion. The total capital costs, and their spread over the 24 month period is estimated as follows.

Table 10.4

Category	Amount	Year 1	Year 2
Pant and machinery	£62.4m	40%	60%
Land purchase	£2.3m	100%	–
Buildings	£14.6m	65%	35%
Start-up expenses	£2.9m	100%	–
Total	£82.2m		

In addition to these costs, interest will be capitalized prior to operation of the plant. The plant and machinery is expected to have a life of 20 years, after which time it would have no scrap value, and the building of 50 years. The accounting policy is to depreciate start-up expenses (professional fees, surveys, engineering studies and so on) and capitalized interest over six years. The depreciation policy is to use the straight line method for plant and machinery, buildings, start-up expenses and capitalized interest.

Working capital

The following working capital periods are assumed:

- debtors pay in 30 days
- creditors are paid in 30 days
- stock is held for 30 days.

The proposed financing structure

It is hoped to establish the paper mill operation as a project company (tentatively called GreenNews Ltd) separate from Ecowaste. Ecowaste's own waste paper collection operation would be merged with the new company, for which Ecowaste would receive additional equity in the new company. A high proportion of debt will be used to gear up returns to make the equity sufficiently attractive.

Ecowaste's merchant bankers have discussed the project with a number of interested banks and investors. The consensus appears to be that, subject to satisfactory economic forecasts, debt could be available on the following terms:

- loan life of 12 years maximum
- grace period of 2.5 years
- interest rate of LIBOR + 1.5 per cent
- maximum debt: total funding of 60 per cent

Investors would expect the IRR on equity returns to be 15 per cent in real terms over a 10-year operating period.

DISCUSSION

The overall structure

A worked solution to this case is given in the Appendix to this chapter (see page 185). The model was written in Excel 4, with each module set up as a separate document bound into a single workbook. In Lotus or Quattro Pro terms, this is analogous to a multisheet worksheet. Exactly the same approach would be suitable for any spreadsheet package with similar facilities.

The model comprises of three main sections: data, logic and output. There are five modules within the data section, seven within the logic section and two in the output section. No data is entered into either the logic or output sections. The only formula used in the data section is in cell B13 of sheet 3, which sets the revenue to start two years from the start of construction (which is in sheet 4 cell B11). This formula was used as a matter of convenience to improve readability. The model extends from 1995 to 2010, although it is only printed out up to 2003 for reasons of space.

Each data and logic module has a brief descriptive note at the start. This summarizes the content, purpose, inputs and outputs of each module. Worksheet columns are used for various purposes in data modules, as the need dictates. However, in logic and output modules (with the exception of logic module 2, which is not time-based), columns C onwards are reserved for years. The same columns are used in each module. For example, in all modules, column F is 1998. Column A is used for description and column B for miscellaneous constants. Unless indicated to the contrary, all amounts are shown in £'000s.

The logical flow of the model is from data through logic to output sections. With the single exception referred to above, data sheets do not refer to any other sheets. The logic sheets all refer in some way to data sheets and to output sheets. Most logic sheets refer to logic sheet 1, which is used for intermediate calculations, but not to other logic sheets. The exceptions to this are the working capital calculation (sheet 7), which looks at revenue and cost analyses (sheets 3 and 4), and the finance calculation (sheet 6), which uses figures from the capital costs schedule (sheet 5).

The remainder of this chapter will go through the logic of the model in some detail, focusing on the formulae that are most likely to give problems. In this discussion, cells will be referred to by the convention 'sheet:cell', where sheets are labelled D for data, L for logic, and O for output. Thus, cell D12 on logic sheet 3 will be written L3:cell D12 and row 5 on data sheet 2 as D2:row 5.

Sheet 1 of 7: the working sheet

Content

This module contains miscellaneous intermediate calculations. These are of two kinds: first, results needed by multiple sheets and, second, those to simplify formulae in other sheets. The annual output calculation in row 14 is an example of the former type and the loan repayments in rows 47 and 48 an example of the latter. The individual calculations are discussed next.

The calculations

Annual output (row 14)

THE FORMULA

C14: =if(C23="No",'Data 3'!$B$12, 0)

Note: Excel 4 prefaces cell references that are not in the current sheet with '[filename.xlw] sheet_name'. The file name does not matter here, and so for our purposes it will be ignored and the reference will be solely 'sheet_name'.

DISCUSSION

In this example, the mill output is fixed at 100 000 tonnes per annum. There is, however, the possibility that construction will be delayed and, therefore, production will not commence until later. The purpose of this line, then, is to provide a production figure for each year, linked to the specified mill output (D3:cell B12) and the date that production starts (D3:cell B13).

To do this, the formula references a further calculation (row 23) that is set to 'Yes' if the mill is still under construction and 'No' if not. This formula is looked at next.

Construction flag (row 23)

THE FORMULA

C23: =if('Data 3'!$B$13<=C11, "No", "Yes")

DISCUSSION

This formula looks at the date that production should start and sets a flag depending on whether or not the start date given in Data 3 is greater than the current date. The formula is quite basic and will only work correctly if the date specified is the first day of the year. If, say, 1/7/97 were used instead, the flag is still set to 'Yes': it does not record the fact that there is only a half year's production.

The flag works because the years in L1:row 11 are formatted to a date format. Cell C11, for instance, is actually held as 01-01-1995 formatted as YYYY. This is required so that the formulae in row 23 can compare like with like, that is one date with another. It would also have been possible in this instance, if perhaps slightly less elegant, to make both L1:row 11 and D3:cell B13 formatted as normal numbers. However, while this procedure would work in a simple case such as this, if the rule that production must be in full-year chunks were relaxed, then the date method would be needed.

Inflation indices (rows 17 and 18)

THE FORMULAE

C17: =(1+'Data 5'!$B$31)^INT((C11-DATE(1994,1,1))/365)

C18: =(1+'Data 5'!$B$32)^INT((C11-DATE(1994,1,1))/365)

DISCUSSION

These two formulae are functionally identical, the difference between them being the data cell they reference. Their purpose is to turn the annual inflation rates into a time series of indices to be used by the operating cost and revenue logic modules.

Each formula can be split into two parts (cell C17 will be used to illustrate). The first part, (1+'Data 5'!$B$31), extracts the inflation percentage from the data module. The second part, INT((C11-DATE(1994,1,1))/365), raises it to a power, such that in 1995 (column C) the formula used is 1.03^1. This means that, as prices are in 1994 terms, by 1995 there has been one year's inflation.

Escalated input prices (rows 31 to 38)

THE FORMULAE

C32: ='Data 1'!$B24*C$18
C33: ='Data 1'!$B25*C$18
C34: ='Data 1'!$B26*C$18

C36: ='Data 2'!$B36*C$18
C37: ='Data 2'!$B37*C$18
C38: ='Data 2'!$B38*C$18

DISCUSSION

These formulae are quite straightforward; they simply inflate input prices by the indices calculated above (cell C18). The '$' signs enable the same formula to be copied and remain correct. This is an example of a calculation used to simplify formulae in later sections.

Escalated variable operating costs (rows 42 to 44)

THE FORMULAE

B42: =SUM('Data 2'!$B$52:$B$56)
B43: =B42*(1+'Data 2'!$B$60)

C42: =$B42*C$18
C43: =$B43*C$18
C44: =IF(C14>40000, IF(C14<60000,C43,C42),
        IF(C23="No",NA(),0))

DISCUSSION

These are the equivalent of the previous formulae, but for variable costs. The complication in this case is that variable costs are not linearly related to output over all values. Therefore, the formula must check to see what level output is running at in a year. As already noted, output is unlikely to be altered in this model, but the facility to change costs with output may, nevertheless, be a useful one for future developments of the logic.

The formula in column B42 sums all the unit variable costs for output over 60 000 tonnes per annum. Cell B43 then escalates this by 12 per cent for outputs below 60 000 tonnes. The cells to the right of these, that is, from column C onwards, simply escalate these base values. The final row, row 44, then checks which set of numbers to use based on the output calculated in L1: row 14.

C44 does two things. First, provided production is over 40 000 tonnes and as such the variable cost calculation is valid, it selects which of the two rows – rows 42 and 43 – to use. Second, if production is less than 40 000 tonnes, and provided that the plant is not still being built, it flags an error by returning the not applicable function: na(). This will warn users that the bounds of the formula have been exceeded.

Loan repayments (rows 47 and 48)

THE FORMULAE

C47: 1 (input)
D47: =C47+1

C48: IF(C47<='Data 5'!$B$14, IF(C47<='Data 5'!$B$15,"Grace", "Repay"),"Over")

DISCUSSION

These formulae are used to simplify the workings of the financing module (logic 6). One of the conditions of the loan is that repayments do not have to be made for three years subsequent to the loan starting. The formula in C48 tests to see if the grace period is over and repayments should start (based on the period given in D5: Cell B15) and it also tests whether or not repayments have finished (based on the loan life given in D5:Cell B14). A simplification of the formula is that it assumes that the loan begins at the start of the model period.

Sheet 2 of 7: The calculation of current profitability

Content

The purpose of this sheet is slightly different to that of the rest of the logic modules in that it does not solely relate to the proposed new mill, but also to the current recycling activities. The purpose of the sheet is to calculate the cost and revenues, and, hence, profit, related to these activities in the last year. The profit figure produced is useful for comparison with the profits for the new venture, while the costs and revenues are picked up by subsequent modules.

The calculations

Operating costs (rows 12 to 16)

THE FORMULAE

C12: ='Data 1'!B24/1000*'Data 1'!B29
C13: ='Data 1'!B25/1000*'Data 1'!B30
C14: ='Data 1'!B26/1000*'Data 1'!B31
C15: =SUM('Data 1'!$B$15:$B$21)
C16: =SUM(B12:B15)

DISCUSSION
The formulae in rows 12 through to 14 work out the total cost of each type
of waste, simply as cost per tonne multiplied by tonnage collected. The formula in row 15 sums the fixed costs and row 16 totals all costs.

Depreciation (rows 19 to 21)

THE FORMULAE

C19: ='Data 1'!$B$34
C20: =E32
C21: =SUM(B19:B20)

DISCUSSION
This section contains two cross-references to other sections. Row 19 pulls a
number out of the data section, while row 20 refers to a calculation below.
The calculation that feeds into C20 is discussed below.

Lorry depreciation (rows 30 to 33)

THE FORMULAE

B32: =1-(('Data 1'!$B$39/'Data 1'!$B$38)^(1/'Data 1'!$B$40))

C30: 0 (input)
D30: =C33

C31: ='Data 1'!$B$38
D31: 0 (input)

C32: =SUM(C30:C31)*$B$32
C33: =C30+C31-C32

DISCUSSION

This section calculates the reducing balance depreciation on the lorries. It is mostly self-explanatory, apart from the formula in B32, which is itself used in C32 to E32. Written more clearly this formula is:

$$= 1 - \sqrt[4]{\frac{Scrap}{Cost}}$$

which, when applied to the purchase cost of the machines gives a depreciation charge sufficient to reduce the balance to the scrap (resale) value over four years.

Sheet 3 of 7: the cost forecasts for the new mill

Content

This module calculates the operating costs for the new mill, which involves three processes. These are first, summing the fixed costs, second, escalating these costs into nominal terms and, third, calculating variable costs based on the production figures in L1:row 14. It should be noted that, although the non-raw material variable costs will vary with changes in production, the model implicitly assumes that the contracts for supply of raw materials are fixed and do not vary with output. Therefore, if output fell, the raw material costs would remain constant. In practice, if the model was to examine different output scenarios, this point would clearly become very important.

The calculations

Fixed costs (rows 14 to 17)

THE FORMULAE

B14: ='Logic 2'!$B$15
C14: =IF('Logic 1'!C$23="No",$B14*'Logic 1'!C$18,0)

B16: =SUMPRODUCT('Data 2'!$B$14:$B$19, 'Data 2'
    !$C$14:$C$19)/1000
C16: =IF('Logic 1'!C$23="No", $B16*'Logic 1'!C$18, 0)

B17: =SUM('Data 2'!$B$24:$B$26)
C17: =IF('Logic 1'!C$23="No", $B17*'Logic 1'!C$18, 0)

DISCUSSION

There are two types of fixed cost: those from the existing warehouse operation, which are picked up in cell B14, and those from the new mill. Row 14,
from column C onwards, then checks that construction is over (as staff are
assumed to be employed only once the mill is built) and, if it is, escalates the
base value appropriately for each year.

The mill's fixed costs split into two parts: staff and other. Row 16 calculates staff costs. The formula in B16 multiplies the column of staff numbers
in D2:column B by the column of staff costs in the next column. It is a
shorthand way of multiplying $(80 \times 12) + (7 \times 15.75) + ... + (3 \times 10)$. C16 is
a copy of cell C14, as is C17. Cell B17 simply sums the other fixed costs.

Raw material costs (rows 26 to 32)

THE FORMULAE

B26: ='Data 1'!B29
C26: =IF('Logic 1'!C$23="No", $B26*'Logic 1'!C32/1000, 0)

B30: ='Data 2'!B45
C30: =IF('Logic 1'!C$23="No", $B30*'Logic 1'!C36/1000, 0)

DISCUSSION

These formulae are straightforward. The cells in column B copy the ton-
nages of each raw material from either data 1 or data 2, depending on
whether or not it is an existing or a new contract. Cells C26 and C30 then
check that construction is over and, if it is, return the cost in nominal terms.

Other variable costs (rows 36 and 40)

THE FORMULAE

C36: ='Logic 1'!C44/1000*'Logic 1'!C14

B40: ='Data 2'!$C$20
C40: =MAX(0, ('Logic 1'!C$14-'Data 2'!$E$20)*$B$40)*
  'Logic 1'!C$21/1000 * 'Data 2'!$B$19

DISCUSSION

The formula in cell C36 multiplies the unit operating cost by production,
both from logic module 1. The formulae in row 40 are concerned with the
calculation of sales commission. Cell B40 copies the rate of commission
from data 2. Cell C40 contains the calculation. C40 is the product of three
parts, as follows:

- MAX(0, ('Logic 1'!C$14-'Data 2'!$E$20)*$B$40) – the first part of the formula, then, calculates the difference between current production and the 80 000-tonne starting point for commission, which is then multiplied by the rate
- 'Logic 1'!C$21/1000 – this is the selling price per tonne
- 'Data 2'!$B$19 – and this is the number of sales staff.

Sheet 4 of 7: the revenue forecasts for the new mill

Content

This module performs only one calculation, which is a simple multiplication to derive annual revenue. Despite the simplicity, it is important to keep it as a separate sheet and not, say, include the calculation in the cash flow sheet. Then if further complexities are added at a later stage, they can be incorporated easily. It also makes for a neater, more understandable and, therefore, less error-prone, model.

The calculations

Net revenue (row 12)

THE FORMULA

C12: ='Logic 1'!C14*'Logic 1'!C21/1000

DISCUSSION

The calculation is tonnage (L1:cell C14) multiplied by the selling price in £'000s (L1:cell C21).

Sheet 5 of 7: the capital costs and depreciation

Content

This module maintains records of assets and calculates depreciation charges by asset type. It is quite a long module and perhaps seems to be rather a lot of trouble to go to simply to calculate one line of the profit and loss account, but the work done here enables a balance sheet to be added to the model quite simply. The method of calculating depreciation so that different asset lives are automatically recognized by the model is worth close investigation as it is a useful approach.

The calculations

Warehouse buildings (row 13)

THE FORMULA

C13: ='Data 1'!$B$34

DISCUSSION

This is simply a copy from data 1. It is assumed, with the lack of information to the contrary, that this depreciation charge carries on for the life of the model.

Land (rows 18 to 20)

THE FORMULAE

C18: 0 (input)
D18: =C20
C19: ='Data 4'!D$16*'Data 4'!$B$16
C20: =C18+C19

DISCUSSION

Land is not depreciated and, therefore, this schedule is included for complete-ness only. The formula in C19 multiplies the total cost of land purchased by the percentage of that cost expected to fall in 1995. This enables capital costs to be split in different ways across the years. This could be used, for example, to model 'soft' payment terms on plant and machinery.

These calculations are identical to the subsequent schedules for plant and machinery, buildings and so on. Therefore, the formulae are not repeated.

Plant and machinery (rows 23 to 40)

THE FORMULAE

C28: =IF('Logic 1'!C$23="No", (C25-C40)/'Data 4'!$B$24, 0)
C37: =IF(AND('Logic 1'!B$23="Yes" ,'Logic 1'!C$23="No"),C25 ,0)
C39: =IF(C37<>0, C38, 0)
C40: =MAX($B40:B40, IF(SUM($C39:$R39)+'Data 4'!$B$24=C38,
        SUM($C37:$R37), 0))

DISCUSSION

The purpose of these formulae (which are also used by all subsequent sched-ules) is to calculate the annual depreciation charge until the asset is fully depreciated. It assumes that all purchases are made at the start of the year, but that depreciation does not start until the mill has been completed.

Row 28 calculates the depreciation for the year. Cell C28 checks that construction is over and, if it is, calculates depreciation as the book value of assets in the year less the cumulative value of assets already fully depreciated. The calculation of assets that are fully depreciated is made in rows 37 to 40.

Row 37 returns the book value of assets in the year after construction finishes. It determines when this is by testing when construction was taking place in the prior year, but not in the current year. Row 38 is a counter, which increments from 1 in C38 by 1 each year. Row 39 checks which year row 37 has returned a non-zero number for, then itself returns the number of the counter for that year. Row 40 then uses this to log whether the assets are fully depreciated. It does this by testing whether the number in row 39 plus the depreciation period equals the current year counter. If it does, it returns the value from row 37. The MAX statement ensures that depreciation does not start again.

Sheet 6 of 7: financing

Content

This section calculates how much debt and equity will be required to finance the given capital expenditure (capex) and what the repayments and interest will be on the debt portion. For the sake of simplicity no finance fees have been assumed in this example. The major difficulty then is how to calculate capitalized interest, which should include interest on itself and still keep the debt ratio correct.

The calculations

Equity (rows 14 and 15) and debt (rows 20 to 26)

THE FORMULAE

C14: =(1-'Data 5'!$B$22)*('Logic 5'!C$87+C23)
C15: =B15+C14

B20: ='Data 5'!$B$26+'Data 5'!$B$16

C22: ='Logic 5'!C$87-C14
C23: =C22/(1-$B$20)-C22
C24: =IF('Logic 1'!C$48="Repay", MAX($B26:B26)/('Data 5'!$B$14-'Data 5'!$B$15), 0)
C25: =IF(ROUND(C23,6)=0, (C20+SUM(C22:C23))*$B$20, 0)

DISCUSSION

Both equity and debt are considered together here as they are obviously interrelated. The best starting point is the drawing on debt and issue of equity. In this example the target debt/(debt+equity) ratio is 50 per cent. As capex is £39.65 million in 1995, equity might be expected to be £19.83 million in that year. However, this fails to take account of the capitalized interest on debt. Therefore, the objectives that have to be fulfilled are:

- raise sufficient total funding to pay for capex and capitalized interest
- make equity 50 per cent of this total
- include interest on the capitalized interest.

This is an iterative process, that is, it will produce a CIRCular reference on a spreadsheet. It will, however converge (that is, produce a stable solution) if set up in the correct way. The formula for issue of equity provides a starting point as it takes the product of 1-gearing ratio and the sum of capital expenditure plus capitalized interest. Drawings on debt for capital expenditure are then set to fund the capex that is not funded by equity. The capitalized interest is then calculated as:

$$\frac{debt}{(1 - \text{interest rate})} - debt$$

This formula (which was discussed further in Chapter 5) calculates the interest on the capitalized interest on the interest and so on, such that the final charge is correct.

Cell C24 calculates when repayments should be made, taking into account the grace periods and loan life entered in data 5. It is flexible enough to detect how much the maximum loan to be repaid is. Cell C25 calculates interest to be paid, checking that interest is only paid if capitalization has first stopped.

Sheet 7 of 7: the working capital

This module calculates the amount of working capital for use by the cash flow. It is in three parts: debtors, creditors and stocks. In each case, the closing balance calculation is of the form (days/365) × £, where £ is the revenue for debtors, operating costs for creditors and output-related costs (materials) for stocks.

CONCLUSION

This chapter has concentrated on a fairly straightforward example. It has, however, illustrated many of the most common problems that are encountered in financial modelling. The aim of the approach to solving these has tried to be clear at all times and choose the most obvious way of working when this has been acceptable. Even with this aim though, some formulae are inevitably still quite complicated. Indeed, it may be thought that some parts of the model are more complicated than they need be. For example, why should depreciation be able to cope with different asset lives? It will always be a moot point how flexible a model should be and that is a difficult question to answer. Nevertheless, building a model with as much regard as possible to its future use will always be an important part of making a model that is error-free and will remain so.

APPENDIX: THE WORKED SOLUTION TO THE ECOWASTE EXAMPLE

	A	B	C
1	**DATA 1 OF 5: EXISTING OPERATIONS**		
2			
3			
4	**Notes**		
5	*Contents* Economic data on existing waste collection operations.		
6	*Purpose* Hold information about existing waste management operations.		
7	*Inputs* Data from 1993 management report ref. CDV/21.		
8	*Outputs* Logic 1, 2, 3, 5.		
9	*NB* Data all refers to period 1/1/93–31/12/93.		
10			
11			
12	*Operating costs*		
13			
14	*Cost category*	*£'000*	
15	heat and light	10.11	
16	staff	32.47	
17	business rates	7.20	
18	machinery maintenance	1.89	
19	building maintenance	2.01	
20	consumables	4.98	
21	lorry running costs	175.00	(7 lorries, £25,000 per annum each)
22			
23	*Cost of waste*	*£/tonne*	
24	newspaper publishers	£33.42	
25	local councils	£28.50	
26	direct collection	£27.70	
27			
28	*Tonnage of waste*	*Tonnes*	
29	newspaper publishers	45 000	
30	local councils	25 700	
31	direct collection	25 600	
32			
33	*Depreciation*	*£'000*	
34	building depreciation	25.00	
35			

	A	B	C	-
36	lorry depreciation			
37	purchase date		01-Jan-91	
38	purchase price		490.00	
39	resale value		210.00	
40	life		4 years	
41				
42				
43	*Revenue*			
44				
45	Tonnage sold		96,300	
46	Average price per tonne		£49.00	

	A	B	C	D	E	F
1	**DATA 2 OF 5: OPERATING COSTS (NEW MILL)**					
2						
3						
4	**Notes**					
5	*Contents* operating cost data at 1/1/94 prices.					
6	*Purpose* Hold basic data that will subsequently be used for					
7	forecasting purposes.					
8	*Inputs* Data from PaperCons' technical report ref. PC324/z.					
9	*Outputs* Logic 1, 3.					
10						
11						
12	*Fixed costs: staff*					
13			*Numbers*	*Av. cost*		
14	Production staff		80	12,000		
15	Supervisors		7	15,750		
16	Maintenance		12	13,000		
17	Management		3	25,000		
18	Administration		6	13,800		
19	Sales: basic		3	10,000		
20	commission			0.25% of sales over 80 000 tonnes		
21						
22	*Fixed costs: other*					

	A	B	C	D	E	F
23			*£'000s*			
24	Vehicle leases		1 380			
25	Business rates		500			
26	Office costs		40			
27						
28	*Raw material volumes*					
29	(per 1 tonne of newsprint produced)					
30			*Tonnes*			
31	Waste paper		1.174			
32	Pulp		0.22119			
33						
34	*Additional waste contracts: prices*					
35			*£/tonne*			
36	Newspaper publisher		£35.00			
37	Local councils		£28.50			
38	Pulp		£300.00			
39						
40						
41						
42						
43	*Additional waste contracts: volumes*					
44			*Tonnes*			
45	Newspaper publisher		15,000			
46	Local councils		6,100			
47	Pulp		22,119			
48						
49	*Other variable costs (60 000 to 100 000 tonnes output)*					
50			*£/tonne of*			
51			*newsprint*			
52	Fuel oil		£12.03			
53	Electricity		£24.19			
54	Chemicals		£38.41			
55	Maintenance		£7.50			
56	Other consumables		£24.33			
57						
58	*Other variable costs (40 000 to 59 999 tonnes output)*					
59						
60	Premium over above figures		12%			

	A	B	C	D	E	F	G
1	\multicolumn{7}{l}{DATA OF 3 OF 5: REVENUE (NEW MILL)}

1 DATA OF 3 OF 5: REVENUE (NEW MILL)

2

> **Notes**
>
> *Contents* Data on production volumes and selling price.
> *Purpose* Drive revenue calculation.
> *Inputs* PaperCons' technical report ref. PC324/z and Ecowaste price survey.
> *Outputs* Logic 1.

(rows 3–9)

10

11	*Planned output*				
12	Volume		100,000	tonnes/year	
13	Start date		01-Jan-97	(fixed to be 2 years from	
				start of construction)	
14					
15	*Selling price*				
16	Gross		£375	per tonne	
17	Less delivery		£20	per tonne	

	A	B	C	D	E	F	G

1 DATA 4 OF 5: CAPITAL COSTS (NEW MILL)

2

3

> **Notes**
>
> *Contents* Capital costs for new mill.
> *Purpose* Hold data on construction cost of mill.
> *Inputs* Data from PaperCons' technical report ref. PC324/z.
> *Outputs* Data 3, Logic 5.

(rows 4–9)

10

11 Start of construction 01-Jan-95

12

13 *Capital costs*

	A	B	C	D	E	F	G
14					*Allocation*		
15			*£'000s*	*1995*	*1996*	*1997*	*1998*
16	land purchase		2,300	100%			
17	Plant and machinery		62,400	40%	60%		
18	Buildings		14,600	65%	35%		
19	Start-up expenses		2,900	100%			
20							
21	*Depreciation policy*						
22			*Years*				
23	Land		N/A				
24	Plant and machinery		20				
25	Buildings		50				
26	Start-up expenses		6				
27	Capitalized interest and fees		6				

	A	B	C	D	E
1	**DATA 5 OF 5: FINANCING AND ECONOMIC ASSUMPTIONS**				
2					
3	**Notes**				
4	*Contents* Indicative financing data.				
5	*Purpose* Hold finance and miscellaneous data.				
6	*Inputs* Advice of Smyth Brothers' merchant bank, based on				
7	soundings of lending and investment institutions carried out				
8	April 1994.				
9	*Outputs* Logic 1, 6, 7.				
10					
11	*Indicative loan terms*				
12					
13	Terms				
14	Loan life	12	years		
15	Grace period	3	years		
16	Margin over LIBOR	1.50%			
17					
18	Covenants				
19	Debt/total funding 60% maximum				
20					
21	Assumptions used				
22	Debt/total funding	50%			
23					
24	*Economic estimates*				
25					
26	LIBOR 8% over project life				
27	Selling price inflation 3% over project life				
28	Operating cost inflation 3% over project life				
29					
30					
31	*Working capital assumptions*				
32					
33	Debtors	30	days		
34	Creditors	30	days		
35	Stock	30	days		

	A	B	C	D	E	F	G	H	I	J	K
1	**LOGIC 1 OF 7: WORKING SHEET**										
2											
3	**Notes**										
4	*Contents* Miscellaneous intermediate calculations.										
5	*Purpose* Hold calculations required by several modules, so as to simplify formulae in other sheets.										
6	*Inputs* Data 1, 2, 3, 5.										
7	*Output* Logic 3, 4, 6.										
8											
9											
10											
11	*(£'000s)*		1995	1996	1997	1998	1999	2000	2001	2002	2003
12											
13	*Annual output*										
14	Production (tonnes)		0	100,000	100,000	100,000	100,000	100,000	100,000	100,000	100,000
15											
16	*Inflation indices*										
17	Income		1.03	1.06	1.09	1.13	1.16	1.19	1.23	1.27	1.30
18	Operating costs		1.03	1.06	1.09	1.13	1.16	1.19	1.23	1.27	1.30
19											
20	*Selling price*										
21	In nominal terms				£387.92	£399.56	£411.54	£423.89	£436.61	£449.70	£463.19
22											
23	*Construction?*		Yes	Yes	No	No	No	No	No	No	No
24											

A	B	C	D	E	F	G	H	I	J	K
25 LOGIC 1 OF 7: WORKING SHEET										
26										
27										
28 (£'000s)		1995	1996	1997	1998	1999	2000	2001	2002	2003
29										
30 *Escalated input prices (£/tonne)*										
31 Waste paper (existing contracts)										
32 publishers		£34.42	£35.46	£36.52	£37.61	£38.74	£39.91	£41.10	£42.34	£43.61
33 local councils		£39.36	£30.24	£31.14	£32.08	£33.04	£34.03	£35.05	£36.10	£37.19
34 direct collection		£28.55	£29.39	£30.27	£31.18	£32.11	£33.08	£34.07	£35.09	£36.14
35 Waste paper (new contracts)										
36 publishers		£36.05	£37.13	£38.25	£39.39	£40.57	£41.79	£43.05	£44.34	£45.67
37 local councils		£29.36	£30.24	£31.14	£32.08	£33.04	£34.03	£35.05	£36.10	£37.19
38 Pulp @ £300 per tonne		£309.00	£318.27	£327.82	£337.65	£347.78	£358.22	£368.96	£380.03	£391.43
39										
40 *Escalated variable operating costs*										
41	Base									
42 If output >= 60 000 tonnes (£/tonne)	£106.46	£109.65	£112.94	£116.33	£119.82	£123.42	£127.12	£130.93	£134.86	£138.91
43 If output < 60 000 tonnes (£/tonne)	£119.24	£122.81	£126.50	£130.29	£134.20	£138.23	£142.37	£146.64	£151.04	£155.57
44 Cost to use		£0.00	£0.00	£116.33	£119.82	£123.42	£127.12	£130.93	£134.86	£138.91
45										
46 *Loan repayments*										
47 Years from start		1	2	3	4	5	6	7	8	9
48 repay?		Grace	Grace	Grace	Repay	Repay	Repay	Repay	Repay	Repay

	A	B	C	D	E	F	G
1	**LOGIC 2 OF 7: CALCULATION OF CURRENT PROFITABILITY**						
2							
3	**Notes**						
4	*Contents* Calculation of costs and revenues of current operations.						
5	*Purpose* Calculate existing profitability as a comparator against which the proposed project can be assessed.						
6	*Inputs* Data 1						
7	*Outputs* None – calculation is for information only.						
8	*NB*: Profitability is for the year ended 31/12/93.						
9							
10	Operating costs						
11	Waste	£'000s					
12	newspaper publishers	1,503.90					
13	local councils	732.45					
14	direct collection	709.12					
15	other	233.66					
16	Total	3,179.13					
17							
18	*Depreciation*						
19	Buildings	25.00					
20	Lorries (see below)	61.23					
21		86.23					
22							
22							
23	*Total costs*	3,265.37					
24							

	A	B	C	D	E	F	G
25	**LOGIC 2 OF 7: CALCULATION OF CURRENT PROFITABILITY**						
26							
27							
28	*Lorry depreciation schedule*						
29		*Rate*	*1991*	*1992*	*1993*		
30	Balance B/Fwd		0.00	396.46	320.78		
31	purchases		490.00	0.00	0.00		
32	depreciation charge	19.09%	93.54	75.68	61.23		
33	Balance C/Fwd		396.46	320.78	259.55		
34							
35	*Revenue*	*4,718.70*					
36							
37							
38	*Profit for 1993*	*1,453.33*					

	A	B	C	D	E	F	G	H	I	J	K
1	**LOGIC 3 OF 7: COST FORECASTS (NEW MILL + WASTE OPS)**										
2											
3		**Notes**									
4		*Contents* Calculation of operating costs over planning period.									
5		*Purpose* Translate cost data into forecasts.									
6		*Inputs* Data 1, 2, logic 1.									
7		*Outputs* Logic 7, outputs 1 and 2									
8		*NB:* 'Base' figures are in 1/1/94 prices; all others are in nominal terms.									
9											
10											
11	(*£'000s*)		*Base*	*1995*	*1996*	*1997*	*1998*	*1999*	*2000*	*2001*	*2002*	*2003*
12											
13	*Fixed costs*										
14	Warehouse		234	0	0	255	263	271	279	287	296	305
15	New mill										
16	Staff (excluding sales commission)		1,414	0	0	1,545	1,592	1,639	1,688	1,739	1,791	1,845
17	Other		1,920	0	0	2,098	2,161	2,226	2,293	2,361	2,432	2,505
18											

LOGIC 3 OF 7: COST FORECASTS (NEW MILL + WASTE OPS)

A	B	C	D	E	F	G	H	I	J	K
19 LOGIC 3 OF 7: COST FORECASTS (NEW MILL + WASTE OPS)										
20										
21										
22 (£'000s)	Base	1995	1996	1997	1998	1999	2000	2001	2002	2003
23										
24 Raw material costs										
25 Waste paper (existing contracts)	tonnes									
26 publishers @ £33.42 per tonne	45,000	0	0	1,643	1,693	1,743	1,796	1,850	1,905	1,962
27 local councils @ £28.5 per tonne	25,700	0	0	800	824	849	875	901	928	956
28 direct collection @ £27.7 per tonne	25,600	0	0	775	798	822	847	872	898	925
29 Waste paper (new contracts)										
30 publishers @ £35 per tonne	15,000	0	0	574	591	609	627	646	665	685
31 local councils @ £28.5 per tonne	6,100	0	0	190	196	202	208	214	220	227
32 Pulp @ £300 per tonne	22,119	0	0	7,251	7,469	7,693	7,923	8,161	8,406	8,658
33										
34 Other variable costs										
35										
36 Output-related		0	0	11,633	11,982	12,342	12,712	13,093	13,486	13,891
37										
38	% of sales									
39	over £80k									
40 Sales-related commission	0.25%	0	0	58	60	62	64	65	67	69
41										
42 Total operating costs		0	0	26,823	27,628	28,457	29,310	30,190	31,095	32,028

	A	B	C	D	E	F	G	H	I	J	K
1	**LOGIC 4 OF 7: REVENUE FORECASTS (NEW MILL)**										
2											
3	Notes										
4	*Contents* Calculation of revenue.										
5	*Purpose* Forecast forward.										
6	*Inputs* Logic 1.										
7	*Outputs* Logic 7, outputs 1 and 2.										
8											
9											
10	*(£'000s)*		*1995*	*1996*	*1997*	*1998*	*1999*	*2000*	*2001*	*2002*	*2003*
11											
12	New revenue		0	0	38,792	39,956	41,154	42,389	43,661	44,970	46,319

	A	B	C	D	E	F	G	H	I	J	K
1	LOGIC 5 OF 7: CAPITAL COSTS AND DEPRECIATION										
2											
3	Notes										
4	*Contents* Schedules of equity and debt.										
5	*Purpose* Calculate debt: equity mix and debt service payments.										
6	*Inputs* Data 5, logic 1, 5.										
7	*Outputs* Outputs 1, 2										
8											
9											
10	*(£'000s)*		*1995*	*1996*	*1997*	*1998*	*1999*	*2000*	*2001*	*2002*	*2003*
11											
12	*Warehouse assets*										
13	Buildings		25	25	25	25	25	25	25	25	25
14											
15	Mill assets										
16											
17	Land										
18	value at cost b/fwd		0	2,300	2,300	2,300	2,300	2,300	2,300	2,300	2,300
19	purchase		2,300	0	0	0	0	0	0	0	0
20	value at cost c/fwd		2,300	2,300	2,300	2,300	2,300	2,300	2,300	2,300	2,300
21											
22	Plant and machinery										
23	book value b/fwd		0	24,960	62,400	62,400	62,400	62,400	62,400	62,400	62,400
24	additions		24,960	37,440	0	0					

	A	B	C	D	E	F	G	H	I	J	K
25	book value c/fwd	24,960	62,400	62,400	62,400	62,400	62,400	62,400	62,400	62,400	62,400
26											
27	written down value b/fwd		0	24,960	62,400	59,280	56,160	53,040	49,920	46,800	43,680
28	depreciation for year		0	0	3,120	3,120	3,120	3,120	3,120	3,120	3,120
29	written down value c/fwd		24,960	62,400	59,280	56,160	53,040	49,920	46,800	43,680	40,560
30											
31											
32											
33											
34	*(£'000s)*		*1995*	*1996*	*1997*	*1998*	*1999*	*2000*	*2001*	*2002*	*2003*
35											
36	Working calculations										
37	Total amount to depreciate		0	0	62,400	0	0	0	0	0	0
38	Counter		1	2	3	4	5	6	7	8	9
39	Counter to use		0	0	3	0	0	0	0	0	0
40	Amount to fully depreciate		0	0	0	0	0	0	0	0	0
41											
42	*Buildings*										
43	Book value b/fwd		0	9,490	14,600	14,600	14,600	14,600	14,600	14,600	14,600
44	additions		9,490	5,110	0	0					
45	Book value c/fwd		9,490	14,600	14,600	14,600	14,600	14,600	14,600	14,600	14,600
46											
47	Written down value b/fwd		0	9,490	14,600	14,308	14,016	13,724	13,432	13,140	12,848
48	depreciation for year		0	0	292	292	292	292	292	292	292
49	Written down value c/fwd		9,490	14,600	14,308	14,016	13,724	13,432	13,140	12,848	12,556

	A	B	C	D	E	F	G	H	I	J	K
50											
51	Working calculations										
52	Total amount to depreciate		0	0	14,600	0	0	0	0	0	0
53	Counter		1	2	3	4	5	6	7	8	9
54	Counter to use		0	0	3	0	0	0	0	0	0
55	Amount fully depreciated		0	0	0						
56											
57											
58											
59											
60	(£'000s)		*1995*	*1996*	*1997*	*1998*	*1999*	*2000*	*2001*	*2002*	*2003*
61											
62	*Start-up expenses*										
63	Book vaue b/fwd		0	2,900	2,900	2,900	2,900	2,900	2,900	2,900	2,900
64	additions	2,900		0	0						
65	Book value c/fwd		2,900	2,900	2,900	2,900	2,900	2,900	2,900	2,900	2,900
66											
67	Written down value b/fwd		2,900	2,900	2,900	2,417	1,933	1,450	967	483	0
68	depreciation for year		0	0	483	483	483	483	483	483	0
69	Written down value c/fwd		2,900	2,900	2,417	1,933	1,450	967	483	0	0
70											
71	Working calculations										
72	Total amount to depreciate		0	0	2,900	0	0	0	0	0	0
73	Counter		1	2	3	4	5	6	7	8	9

A	B	C	D	E	F	G	H	I	J	K
74 Counter to use	0	0	0	3	0	0	0	0	0	0
75 Amount fully depreciated	0	0	0	0	0	0	0	0	0	2,900
76										
77										
78										
79										
80 *Capitalized interest and fees*										
81 Book value b/fwd		0	1,977	4,099	4,099	4,099	4,099	4,099	4,099	4,099
82 Additions		1,977	2,122	0	0	0	0	0	0	0
83 Book value c/fwd		1,977	4,099	4,099	4,099	4,099	4,099	4,099	4,099	4,099
84										
85 Written down value b/fwd		0	1,977	4,099	3,416	2,733	2,050	1,366	683	0
86 depreciation		0	0	683	683	683	683	683	683	0
87 Written down value c/fwd		1,977	4,099	3,416	2,733	2,050	1,366	683	0	0
88										
89 *Working calculations*										
90 Total amount to depreciate		0	0	4,099	0	0	0	0	0	0
91 Counter		1	2	3	4	5	6	7	8	9
92 Counter to use		0	0	3	0	0	0	0	0	0
93 Amount fully depreciated		0	0	0	0	0	0	0	0	4,099
94										
95 *Total capital expenditure*		39,650	42,550							
96 (excluding capitalized interest and fees)										

LOGIC 6 OF 7: FINANCING

Notes:

Contents Schedules of equity and debt
Purpose Calculate debt: equity mix and debt service payments.
Inputs Data 5, logic 1, 5.
Outputs Outputs 1, 2

A	B	C	D	E	F	G	H	I	J	K
(£'000s)		*1995*	*1996*	*1997*	*1998*	*1999*	*2000*	*2001*	*2002*	*2003*
Equity										
Amount issued		20,814	22,336	0	0	0	0	0	0	0
Cumulative		20,814	43,150	43,150	43,150	43,150	43,150	43,150	43,150	43,150
Debt										
		Rate								
		9.5%								
Balance b/fwd		0	20,814	43,150	43,150	38,355	33,561	28,766	23,972	19,178
drawings for:										
capital expenditure		18,836	20,214	0	0	0	0	0	0	0
capitalized interest		1,977	2,122	0	0	0	0	0	0	0
principal repayments		0	0	0	4,794	4,794	4,794	4,794	4,794	4,794
interest paid		0	0	4,099	4,099	3,644	3,188	2,733	2,277	1,822
Balance c/fwd		20,814	43,150	43,150	38,355	33,561	28,766	23,972	19,178	14,383
Actual debt/(debt + equity) ratio		50.0%	50.0%	50.0%	47.1%	43.8%	40.0%	35.7%	30.8%	25.0%

LOGIC 7 OF 7: WORKING CAPITAL

Notes

Contents Calculation of debtors, creditors and stock.

Purpose Provide figures for cash flow.

Inputs Data 5, logic 3, 4.

Ouputs Output 1

(£'000s)	1995	1996	1997	1998	1999	2000	2001	2002	2003
Debtors									
Opening balance	0	0	0	3,188	3,284	3,383	3,484	3,589	3,696
Closing balance	0	0	3,188	3,284	3,383	3,484	3,589	3,686	3,807
net increase/(decrease)	0	0	3,188	96	99	101	105	108	111
Creditors									
Opening balance	0	0	0	2,205	2,271	2,339	2,409	2,481	2,556
Closing balance	0	0	2,205	2,271	2,339	2,409	2,481	2,556	2,632
net increase/(decrease)	0	0	2,205	66	68	70	72	74	77
Stocks									
Opening balance	0	0	0	956	985	1,014	1,045	1,076	1,108
Closing balance	0	0	956	985	1,014	1,045	1,076	1,108	1,142
net increase/(decrease)	0	0	956	29	30	30	31	32	33

1 MILL CASH FLOW

		1995	1996	1997	1998	1999	2000	2001	2002	2003
3 (£'000s)										
5 *Project cash flow*										
6 Operating revenue		0	0	38,792	39,956	41,154	42,389	43,661	44,970	46,319
7 less										
8 Operating costs		0	0	26,823	27,628	28,457	29,310	30,190	31,095	32,028
9 Capital expenditure		39,650	42,550	0	0	0	0	0	0	0
10 Increase/(decrease) in working capital		0	0	1,940	58	60	62	64	66	67
11		(39,650)	(42,550)	10,029	12,270	12,638	13,017	13,407	13,809	14,224
13 *Financed by*										
14 Drawings on debt		20 814	22 366	0	0	0	0	0	0	0
15 Issue of equity		20 814	22 336	0	0	0	0	0	0	0
16 less										
17 Debt repayments		0	0	0	4,794	4,794	4,794	4,794	4,794	4,794
18 debt interest		1,977	2,122	4,099	4,099	3,644	3,188	2,733	2,277	1,822
19		39,650	42,550	(4,099)	(8,894)	(8,438)	(7,983)	(7,527)	(7,072)	(6,616)
21 Net cash flow		0	0	5,930	3,376	4,199	5,034	5,880	6,738	7,607
22 *Cumulative net cash flow*		0	0	5,930	9,305	13,505	18,539	24,419	31,157	38,764

A	B	C	D	E	F	G	H	I	J	K
1 MILL PROFIT AND LOSS ACCOUNT										
2										
3 *(£'000s)*		*1995*	*1996*	*1997*	*1998*	*1999*	*2000*	*2001*	*2002*	*2003*
4										
5 Sales		0	0	38,792	39,956	41,154	42,389	43,661	44,970	46,319
6 less										
7 Operating costs		0	0	26,823	27,628	28,457	29,310	30,190	31,095	32,028
8 Depreciation		0	0	4,579	4,579	4,579	4,579	4,579	4,579	3,412
9 *Operating profit*		0	0	7,390	7,749	8,119	8,500	8,892	9,296	10,879
10										
11 Interest payable		0	0	4,099	4,099	3,644	3,188	2,733	2,277	1,822
12										
13 *Profit after interest*		0	0	3,291	3,650	4,475	5,312	6,159	7,019	9,057

11

USING MODELS FOR DECISION MAKING

INTRODUCTION

The premise behind this book is that a large number of the financial models around today either do not produce accurate results or do not fulfil the requirements of those who commissioned them in the first place. Four reasons were offered as explanation for this failure:

- poor understanding of economic and financial analysis
- inadequate planning and poor design of models
- insufficient discipline in structuring models
- incorrect interpretation of model output.

The first three issues have been discussed in some detail. In a sense, these are essentially the 'science' of financial modelling, while the 'art' is contained in the last issue. A model has been built, it is beautifully structured, takes account of all relevant economic variables and calculates NPV just so. Sadly, there is still one last fence to fall at – the interpretation of its output. This chapter focuses on model interpretation by means of a simple example, outlined below.

BACKGROUND

The example that will be used in this chapter is a restaurant start-up. The purpose of building a financial model is to evaluate whether or not the proposed restaurant is a viable proposition and to assess how much equity the owner would need to inject into the project. The owner is a disillusioned accountant who thinks that she would rather cook good food than cook other peoples' books. She knows all about NPV, but for this venture is happy to rely on the restaurant producing merely an acceptable annual salary for her rather than a large NPV.

The eponymously named restaurant, Rebecca's, aims to serve high-quality food, made from good, fresh ingredients, in pleasant but informal surroundings at reasonable prices. Instead of having a fixed-price menu, the price of each course is fixed with small extra charges for vegetables, bread and coffee. There will also be a service charge.

Rebecca plans to open in Edinburgh, a city in which she has lived for five years and knows well. There are already many restaurants in Edinburgh, including some that operate according to a similar concept to her own. However, the area in which she plans to open, a well-off neighbourhood in the south of the city, appears currently to lack the type of restaurant she has in mind. The target customers for Rebecca's are the local population of young and middle-aged professional people.

Suitable premises have been found – an old shop on the corner of a park – and quotes obtained for the rent, conversion, rates and so on from relevant authorities. She has consulted local employment agencies to determine typical staff rates of pay. The model is complicated by the fact that VAT is payable on all restaurant meals.

BUILDING THE MODEL

Rebecca is initially primarily interested in using the model to examine the operating aspects of the business, as distinct from the capital investment and financing implications. Therefore, she decides that the main things she wants the model to look at are:

- profit per customer
- fixed costs
- covers served – including the build-up as the restaurant becomes established.

It is decided that profit per customer makes a suitable starting point for the model. Rebecca believes that the average price of a full meal at her restaurant should be under £20, including wine, if she is to attract large numbers of her target customers on a regular basis. She also believes that the individual prices of starters, main courses and so on are important and should be below certain values. Based on this, she produces the following estimate.

Table 11.1

Items	Menu prices and costs		
	Basic cost	*Menu price*	*Income*
Starter	£2.00	£3.45	£2.94
Main course	£3.25	£7.45	£6.34
Vegetables	£0.50	£0.50	£0.43
Pudding	£1.00	£1.95	£1.66
Coffee/sweets	£0.75	£0.95	£0.81
Bread	£0.30	£0.65	£0.55
Wine(average cost per person)	£2.48	£3.98	£3.38
Subtotal	£10.28	£18.93	£16.11
Service charge(5%)		£0.95	£0.81
VAT reclaimed on purchases	£1.80		
Total	£8.48	£19.87	£16.91

	Wine prices and costs		
	Cost	*% split*	*Selling price*
Basic wine	£3.95	60%	£6.95
Intermediate wine	£5.95	30%	£8.95
Best wine	£7.95	10%	£10.95

From the above it can be calculated that the profit for a customer having a full meal and half a bottle of wine is £8.43 – more or less 50 per cent gross profit, a figure that is by no means substantial for the restaurant business. Rebecca would obviously be very pleased if *everyone* who came into her restaurant took a full three-course meal with half a bottle of wine, but they will not. For example, some people will opt for just two courses and may not have wine. Therefore, Rebecca assumes that 40 per cent of customers will take the full menu and 60 per cent will miss sweet, coffee and bread. Because of her keen pricing of the wine (fixed £3 mark-up on all bottles), she believes that estimates of wine sales are, if anything, conservative.

Rebecca recalculates her table to produce a profit per customer figure for those taking the smaller meal, as shown in Table 11.2.

In this case, the profit per customer is calculated as being £6.95. This is actually a slightly higher percentage of profit to cost as the margins on the items *not* taken are below the average mark-up across the whole menu. This is a small point, though, that does not worry Rebecca and so she calculates the average profit per customer as the weighted average of £8.43 and £6.95, that is, £7.54.

The next stage is to consider how many people will be served by the restaurant. This will depend on a number of factors, the main one being time

Table 11.2

Items	Menu prices and costs		
	Basic cost	*Menu price*	*Income*
Starter	£2.00	£3.45	£2.94
Main course	£3.25	£7.45	£6.34
Vagetables	£0.50	£0.50	£0.43
Pudding	£0.00	£0.00	£0.00
Coffee/sweets	£0.00	£0.00	£0.00
Bread	£0.00	£0.00	£0.00
Wine(average cost per person)	£2.48	£3.98	£3.38
Subtotal	£8.23	£15.38	£13.09
Service charge(5%)		£0.77	£0.65
VAT reclaimed on purchaes	£1.44		
Total	£6.79	£16.14	£13.74

of the week. However, it is also realized that building up trade will take time and that full utilization cannot be expected immediately. The following estimates are therefore produced, based on a planned 80 covers.

Table 11.3

Day	Monday	Tuesday	Wednesday	Thursday	Friday	Saturday	Sunday
Utilization	Closed	50%	60%	70%	110%	110%	80%

Table 11.4

Month	Month 1	Month 2	Month 3	Month 4	Month 5	Month 6	Thereafter
Utilization	25%	40%	50%	70%	80%	95%	100%

The first table forecasts the percentage of the 80 available covers that are expected to be served each night, once the restaurant is fully established. The second table shows the percentage of these covers that is expected to be served in the restaurant's first few months. Therefore, in month 1, on a Tuesday, it is only expected to serve 10 people (25 per cent of 50 per cent of 80 covers). The utilization rates go above 100 per cent on Friday and Saturday as it is expected that some tables can be rebooked. Rebecca believes these figures to be highly conservative as some London restaurants achieve as much as 300 per cent utilization on Friday nights.

Based on these assumptions, and also assuming each 'month' in the build-up profile to be 4 weeks long, Rebecca achieves the following gross profit forecast.

Table 11.5

Month	Month 1	Month 2	Month 3	Month 4	Month 5	Month 6	Thereafter
Profit	£2895	£4633	£5791	£8107	£9265	£11 002	£11 581

To see how this is calculated, consider month 1. There are 4 weeks in the month and, normally, the restaurant would be expected to be 68.6 per cent full for each week (average of 0, 50, 60, 70, 110, 110 and 80 per cent), but, as it is month 1, it will only achieve 25 per cent of that, that is, 17.2 per cent. Converting this into covers gives an answer of just over 96 covers a week, or 384 in the month. At a profit of £7.54 per cover, this yields £2895 profit for the month.

Having made an initial estimate of her restaurant's gross profit, Rebecca turns her attention to overhead costs to see if the projected gross profitability is sufficient to cover them. For convenience, she has estimated these on an annual basis, as shown below.

Table 11.6

Overhead costs	£
Rates	£6000
Utilities	£5000
Repairs	£7500
Insurance	£5000
Printing	£4000
Professional	£3000
Cleaning	Done by staff
Total	£30 500

In addition to these costs, Rebecca estimates that 80 per cent of customers will pay using a credit card, for which she will have to pay an average charge of 4 per cent of the transaction value to the credit card companies. Finally, she estimates the following staff costs (she will be head cook herself, staff are paid a high basic amount and, therefore, do not take a share of the service charge).

Table 11.7

Staff costs	Number	Basic pay per person	Employer's NI per person	Total cost
Front of house manager	1	£16 000	£2240	£18 240
Waiters	3	£11 000	£1155	£36 465
Cooks	2	£12 000	£1260	£26 520
Kitchen assitant	1	£8000	£688	£8688
Total	8			£89 913

The other fixed costs that Rebecca is concerned with are the financing costs. These are of two sorts:

- charges for the provision of the initial loan that finances the start-up costs
- charges for a working capital facility (bank overdraft) that is used to fund differences in paying for supplies and receiving money from customers and so on.

She estimates that the annual cost of these two facilities will be £44 000 and £7000 per annum, respectively. The start-up loan will be repaid in five years' time.

Putting all these figures together, Rebecca calculates that, in the first year, the restaurant will make a loss, as follows.

Gross profit	£111 179
less credit card charges	£8322
Revised gross profit	£102 857
less	
Overheads	£30 500
Financing	£51 000
Staff costs	£89 913
Net profit/(loss)	*(£68 556)*

ANALYSIS

Based on this initial run of the model, Rebecca's restaurant will make a size-able loss in its first year and, for that matter, in subsequent years. The most common response to a model giving this answer is to start looking for areas to change:

- 'Lets try increasing the price'
- 'How about cutting staff costs – we'll have one fewer cooks and cut everyone's pay by 10 per cent'
- 'Perhaps more people will take the full meal'
- 'Wine is too cheap'
- 'Utilization will be better than this'
- 'We could get 100 covers in that room, not just 80'

and so on. In no time, Rebecca's will be making £50 000 profit in its first year, according to the financial model. Perhaps it is obvious to say that a model can show just about any result desired of it, but this point cannot be stressed often enough. However, it is not just conscious manipulation that models are open to. For example, in this case, Rebecca presumably really believes in her restaurant and so will believe that there must be something wrong with the model if it does not show a profit. This may well be the case, but the art of financial modelling lies in spotting when the *project* does not work, as well as when the *model* does not work. This is illustrated below by looking at Rebecca's restaurant a bit more closely.

Pitfall 1: the model's assumptions hide business assumptions

Every financial model, such as that for Rebecca's restaurant, is composed of a number of assumptions (assumption data was discussed in Chapter 4). One assumption in Rebecca's model is that utilization will mostly be below 100 per cent, that is, there will be little rebooking of tables in the same night. There could be two reasons for this assumption. It could be because Rebecca believes that there will not be sufficient demand to fill more than 80 or so covers in any night, that is, there is a limit placed on demand by forces out-side Rebecca's control. In all probability, this is the assumption that most readers of the model would make. However, it is also possible that the limit is a matter of commercial policy on the part of Rebecca and, in this instance, it is the case.

Rebecca is familiar with the requirements of the professionals that she has targeted. She believes that a key requirement is flexible booking times and unpressurized eating, both of which are best served by single booking of tables. Although this reduces her scope for short-term gain, should demand be sufficient, she hopes that it will help build up a large group of loyal regulars. The fair pricing policy again aims to encourage regular visits.

Faced with a model showing a loss, and looking at the assumptions in the model, it is very easy to forget such business assumptions that underlie the forecasts and to increase utilization rates and make prices less 'friendly'. However, to do so invalidates the results of the model.

Pitfall 2: financial models are (too) rational

Financial models work by turning the real world, with all its complexity and imperfection, into a nice, neat series of logical relationships. For example, Rebecca's model assumes that utilization will steadily build up to a level plateau. She might well perform a number of sensitivities to test what might happen if it does not, but, as was discussed in Chapter 1, these will not give any better idea of whether or not it will happen. She might even get really clever and model the build-up as a series of probability distributions, run many trials of the model, and produce an expected value build-up. All these are rational things to do.

The real world, and the restaurant world more than most, is often *not* rational. Rebecca's might gain rave reviews, its decor just hit the mark with Edinburgh professionals, and its Provençal fish soup attain cult status, but, then again, Provençal fish soup might become the 1990's lasagne and chips overnight and Rebecca' s could be deserted by customers who instead flock to the Thai restaurant across the road. These are questions of style and taste and the financial model is absolutely hopeless at dealing with these qualitative, subjective issues. These very factors could, though, be just about all that matters to the success or otherwise of Rebecca' s restaurant.

Pitfall 3: models are approximations

A model is, by definition, an approximation and simplification of the real world. It achieves this simplification in one of two ways: either by missing out many of the relationships that are present in the real world or by replacing complicated real-world relationships with approximations. The result of this is that a model may not react in the way expected when one variable, or relationship, in the model is changed.

In Rebecca's model, by far the most sensitive variable is the number of covers. If the available covers are increased to 120, from 80, the model will show the restaurant to be hugely successful and Rebecca will be able to retire in the Caribbean within a few years. This may be the correct conclusion, but, if it is, then it is no thanks to the model.

The first reason for this is that cooking for, and serving, an extra 40 covers will require an increase in fixed costs (cooks, waiters and so on). This will reduce the extra profit that is made. Nevertheless, this is an easy factor to build into the model using an '@if' function in a spreadsheet, for example. In a similar vein, there would also be an increase in the capital costs, as a result of fitting out more tables, and so the burden of debt service would rise. Nevertheless, net profit would still be expected to rise, albeit more slowly than in a model with no such relationships built into it at all. As an aside it is also worth noting that the greater fixed cost burden needed for the larger restaurant will also increase Rebecca's risks should demand fall.

A more important criticism of the model is that it says nothing about the availability of demand to fill the extra covers. In the model as it stands, increasing covers by 40 has such a large effect in part because fixed costs do not move, but more because utilisation does not move. In other words increasing capacity is actually increasing demand. Although that is the relationship in the model, it is highly unlikely to be the relationship in the real world.

Pitfall 4: models do not create knowledge

In Chapter 3 where model planning was discussed, it was said that before a financial model is built, other non-modelling options should also be considered. One of the principal reasons for this is that financial models can only analyse *existing* knowledge or information. Although this seems obvious it is common to hear people saying things like 'We'll build a model to tell us what our sales will be', when all they intend to do is input a few guesses about revenue into the model.

Rebecca's model is full of potential traps such as this. For example, it is only too easy to start believing that a menu of the price structure entered into the model really will sell in the volumes proposed. If Rebecca wants to increase her belief in this, she might be better off commissioning market research rather than building a financial model.

Pitfall 5: time scales smooth out lumps

When Rebecca starts her restaurant, it will succeed or fail day to day. People will come and eat, or not, day by day; bills will come in day by day; supplies will be bought day by day. Her model neatly smoothes over this and looks at the first year. True, she has budgeted for some working capital, but the model itself is very little help in telling her when the largest demands on her resources will come, and whether or not she will be able to meet them. This has been the downfall of many businesses, just like Rebecca's.

INDEX